AFRICA TREKS
STORIES OF VICTORY
FROM THE AFRICAN BUSH

GERTRUDE E. GAMMON

Winters Publishing
P.O. Box 501
Greensburg, IN 47240
www.winterspublishing.com
800-457-3230

Scripture quotations taken from The King James Version of the Holy Bible.

Published by:
Winters Publishing
P.O. Box 501
Greensburg, IN 47240
www.winterspublishing.com
800-457-3230

ISBN-10 1-883651-33-6
ISBN-13 978-1-883651-33-6
Library of Congress Control Number: 2008942306

Printed in the United States of America.

TABLE OF CONTENTS

PREFACE

On hearing stories of how the Lord marvelously guided and provided in mission work in South Africa, friends have said, "Why don't you write these down in a book?"

Dwight L. Moody said he would rather encourage ten others to work for the Lord, than to do the work of ten men himself. Books about the work of David Brainard, William Carey, Adoniram Judson, John G. Paton and C. T. Studd were such a tremendous encouragement to me. It was a great joy to make the gospel known in South Africa with The Evangelical Alliance Mission (TEAM) from 1951 until 1988. I trust these simple Africa stories may be used of the Lord to inspire others to eagerly work for Him, too! "The Lord gave the word: great was the company of those that published it" (Psalm 68:11).

I thank the Lord for His wonderful help. He said, "… "My grace is sufficient for thee: for my strength is made perfect in weakness …" (2 Corinthians 12:9). "Now thanks be unto God, which always causeth us to triumph in Christ, and maketh manifest the savour of his knowledge by us in every place" (2 Corinthians 2:14).

ACKNOWLEDGEMENTS

I am so thankful to my brothers and sisters, Robah Kellogg, William and Judy Kellogg, and Marshall and Dorothy Bentsen, and a multitude of other Christian friends, who have been such a blessing to me in my walk with the Lord.

Grace Dove (editing assistance), James and Myrna Ferris, Grant and Patricia Hagen, Keith Hyde, James and Claudia Juhl, Steven, Susan, Matthew, Mia and Micah Knapp, Harold, Rebekah, Sarah, Stephen and Grace Mally, Timothy and Eunice McCalley, Bruce and Ilene Uhlenhopp, Tracy Winters, Judy Woods and other saints in Iowa, and Charleston, Edwards, Glasford and Urbana, Illinois have been especially encouraging in the writing of this simple book.

INTRODUCTION

Farm work is time consuming and wearying. My father would rise early near Laura, Illinois to start milking the cows. Occasionally, it would be 9 p.m. before the day's work was finished. It was very strenuous work; sometimes he would take a nap after breakfast, as well as after our noon meal.

When a child, I used to go out to the pasture at 4 a.m. and bring in the cows, to save my father from that long, tiring walk. One day, I decided it would make the task much easier to ride my horse, Gretchen, quickly round up the cattle, and bring them hurrying in, in front of her. All went well, with much time saved – until we reached the cattle. They were resting at the far end of the pasture – probably happily chewing their cuds as they basked in the soft, green grass. Gretchen and I got to the far outskirts of the herd. I commenced to motion to the cows to get up now, so they could go in for their nice breakfast. They just sat there – entirely at ease, and not intending to change position to leave their enjoyable rest! It was amazing – and very puzzling, until I dismounted and walked amongst them, helping them up, and lifting the little calves and setting them on their way. They understood perfectly when someone was right down where they were, lovingly easing them along.

I thanked the Lord for the great understanding this gave, when there were opportunities to go and live with the Africans in their huts, to make the way to heaven known.

There were weeks of summer vacation from teaching in our South African mission schools. So the Lord helped me to make ten such treks through the years, staying in the kraals a week or two at a time. A kraal is a cluster of grass huts where one family lives.

When my father heard I was going out to live with the people, he sent a letter and included Ezekiel 3:15 – "... I sat where they sat, and remained there ... among them ...". It was interesting in one kraal (and reaching out visiting in others as far as we could go), for there was no stump, piece of wood, or anything like a chair to sit on! For us who are used to sitting on something, it is not so easy to sit only on the ground for ten days. (This is easier to understand if experienced!) But it was utter joy to "… give light to them that sit in darkness …" (Luke 1:79).

I was so happy to receive another encouraging letter from

Swazis make mats to sit and sleep on.

my father saying that about the time I started out on one trek, Donald Grey Barnhouse spoke on the radio on John 1:14 – "… the Word was made flesh, and dwelt among us …". My father wrote,

I do not recall his words, but his thought was that Jesus did not come with the aloofness of royalty, or minister to human needs from the comparative comfort of a mission compound, but shared the depths of human poverty.

The appreciation of the people was precious to see. One

Zulu said, "We are just heathen. She is a Christian. The white child speaks of <u>God</u>."

It was difficult to sleep at one kraal. There was somewhat of a depression in the ground, but moving the sleeping bag over and putting a shoulder into the hollow place did not seem to help. The seven days felt like seven months! When we finally arrived back at our school, I stretched out my sleeping bag to air on a clothesline – and out hopped innumerable fleas!

When we reached the hut a kind family provided for us on another trek, Georgena Cole, a missionary from Canada, first looked all around the ceiling for snakes. There were none. However, one night we were wakened by a very strange sound coming across the floor. We clicked on the flashlight to reveal a wide band of large cockroaches with metallic wings, which rattled loudly as the insects marched rapidly forward in formation. We never saw a parade like that again, because my sister sent an insect repellent. "Blessed be the Lord, who daily loadeth us with benefits, even the God of our salvation ..." (Psalm 68:19).

CHAPTER 1

A CHIEF'S KRAAL

One day, some Swazi Christians and I set out for a chief's kraal. The sun grew hotter, as we walked along through a very isolated area. We came to a very sandy stretch, with a slippery embankment. It was very lonesome in a strange land, away from one's loving family. A tiny girl walked along with us. There was a longing just to

Border post made for King George VI's visit.

even hold someone's hand. It would be such a comfort! The embankment was so steep, the thought came that the little child would be happy to have someone hold her hand, to keep her from sliding down in the hot sand. She was so small, that she was at the back of the group – as it was difficult for her to keep up. I walked slowly, until all the others had passed, except the child; forgetting that an African child unaccustomed to a strange, white person (especially if it were the first day she had ever seen one) would be terrified if one touched her. As I reached down lovingly to help her along, she jerked up her tiny arm, and struck mine with the mightiest blow she could muster. The whack was not felt greatly on the arm, but it pierced my heart – making it easier to understand a little of what the Lord suffered for us. He left the glory of heaven to tread this earth, but those He came to bring salvation to "... smote him" (Luke 22:63). Isaiah 53:5 says, "... he was wounded for our transgressions ...".

Cattle kraal is dark cluster of sticks at right of huts.

The farther we walked, the hotter it became. Had I known how far we were going to go, I could have brought water. Our saliva had become little, white balls. At last, we neared the chief's kraal – situated on a little plateau. A cool breeze blew. We became able to speak again.

"Do you want to see the old one?" queried the chief's headman, as we entered the kraal. The fat, smiling chief sat under a thatched shade behind his "throne," a plank with holes cut in it to hold three supporting sticks in place. We read salvation verses, and asked him if he wanted to receive the Saviour. He just smiled and said, "I am still listening!" A long row of his wives stood by his hut. They were listening, too!

After that seemingly fruitless trip, we took comfort in knowing the Lord promises His word will not return to Him void – it will accomplish His purpose (Isaiah 55:11).

CHAPTER 2

AN AFRICAN BUS

Ida (a six-year-old orphan) and I set out for northern Swaziland to visit in kraals with Swazi Christians there. The only bus went south – to Gollel – and another bus went back up north from there. Gollel was fifty miles away, but the road skirted the mountains – so it was actually fifty-eight miles. The other bus going north made it a journey of 124 miles one way.

Ida (at right) helping weave a basket.

We got on the first bus, called "The Free Will of the Swazis," at its nearest stop – some distance down the road from our mission school. Only Africans were on board. The bus had no real door. The "door" of the bus was the driver's

Road to catch the bus (left). Mhlosheni school (center).

assistant, who stood perpetually in the open doorway. We took a "The Way of Salvation" tract from the stack we carried and handed it to the driver. He looked at it, stood up, turned around, held it up, and said, "This tells the way to heaven! Everyone be sure to get one!" Upon arriving in Swaziland, it became immediately apparent they wanted us there. One preacher said, "If the missionaries left, we would just fight each other."

I turned to Ida sitting beside me and asked, "Have you ever ridden on a bus before?" "No," she replied softly. She clung to our thin, hard one-fourth-inch plywood seat to keep from bouncing off, as the bus vaulted over the high bumps and fell into the deep grooves of the corrugated, red dirt road – which reminds us to cling to the Lord in all the ups and downs of our lives.

The bus was having engine trouble. A runner had already been sent for a substitute bus to come and take over the passengers.

The motor went along fairly well for a while, until we reached a long, steep hill. The engine sputtered to a stop near the top of the hill. The driver told everyone to get out and walk over to the other side of the brow of the hill. He rolled the bus back to a place where he could turn around. He flew back down the hill – getting the engine going again. Then he brought the bus roaring up over the top of the hill, and kept the motor running as we climbed aboard.

ETTC where I taught two years.

We were making good progress, when suddenly, it began to rain. The road was already slippery from previous rains. The bus began to slide. One time, it slid too far, and got stuck in the softer mud along the shoulder.

"All right. Everyone off!" announced the driver. "Oh, no, Nkosazana!" he said, as I rose. (He was calling me "Daughter of the King.") So I had to stay there, while the others went out into the rain. Amongst those getting their clothes soiled with slimy, red mud was Aaron, a student from the Evangelical Teacher Training College, "ETTC," where the motto was "Every Teacher Teaching Christ." Graduates went out, making the gospel known in Zululand schools. Aaron married Saraphina, another of our students. They named their first child "Charles Spurgeon,"

Charles Spurgeon and Saraphina.

because Aaron enjoyed reading that renowned preacher's sermons so much. The men broke off tree branches, set them in front of the tires, and pushed. The Lord helped the bus resume its place on the road, and its journey – until suddenly, the motor stopped, and could not be started again.

Enjoying sweet potatoes at ETTC.

Some dissatisfaction was voiced regarding the delays. So the driver turned around and said anyone who wanted to could get off, and he would refund the money paid for the rest of the trip. There was silence. No one wanted to get off in the rain – there in the wilderness!

We were stalled next to a fragrant forest of wattle trees (used for tanning leather). It was getting dark. People started to go to

An ETTC student's open air Sunday School.

Some ETTC graduates taught in government schools. This school had 500 pupils.

sleep. However, not all – for the silence was broken by the very audible, deep, bass voice of a man in a back seat saying, "Maybe it is because there is a white person riding on this bus that we are having so much trouble!" Snuggling far down in the front corner to get as far as possible out of sight, I was very thankful the driver had

said to sit there near the door. This is a kind custom the people have for seating us, and on that occasion, I found it a strong blessing! I found comfort in remembering Jonah and how the Lord spared him. For after his fellow passengers threw him into the sea during the storm, Jonah said, "When my soul fainted within me I remembered the Lord …" "Salvation is of the Lord …" (Jonah 2:7, 9). Then it was that the Lord spoke to the whale (Matthew 12:40),

Japhet Elephant (L) and Simon Heaven, who taught in a mission school.

and Jonah was delivered up – not into the sea to be drowned, but onto the "dry land" – another miracle; for at least in South Africa, whales cannot come near dry land, as the water is much too shallow there.

Two Swazi girls, sitting across the aisle, began to sing a hymn, which was most reassuring. Then relative quietness prevailed. Early in the morning, the faint sound of an approaching vehicle awakened us. At last, it arrived. It was the substitute "bus!" Actually, it was a long, flat-bodied truck with a large tarpaulin on the back.

We began to disembark, and to crawl in out of the rain and under the tarpaulin. But the driver kindly asked me to sit in the front. He set his large, metal money box on my lap. I praised the Lord the driver knew he could trust a Christian to keep his money, while he was out of sight at the back of the truck! The box had no lock. It was bulging with large, British notes. There were so many, the lid of the box could not close.

The driver resumed his place, and his assistant slid in at the other door. It was quite daylight before we got started, but it was such a blessing to be on the way, as the other bus would leave Gollel for northern Swaziland at 7 a.m.

The motor started, and we were off. When we reached the foot of a mountain to climb, some maneuvering was required to change gears. First, we had to lift our feet. Then, the assistant raised the thin, plywood floor. He quickly pushed the gears into mesh – before the floor and our feet went down again, so the truck could start climbing the mountain. These actions were repeated eight more times before we reached Gollel.

Usually in making the trip, we stayed overnight with the African preacher's family in their Gollel kraal. But this time, we had stayed in a bus, by a wattle forest. Now, all we needed to do was to reach Gollel before the other bus left. There would not be another bus for several days! At last, we crawled up over the top of the last big hill, and there stood the other bus, with smoke spewing out of its exhaust pipe, ready to take off!

We praised the Lord for His wonderful help, and slipped off

the substitute "bus" onto a real one. Far in the north, we reached our destination. The bus stop was a place where people brought milk to sell. Eight or ten people had gathered there. They seemed amazed to see a white person, and listened, spellbound, as the Lord helped Swazi words come out of a white person's mouth. What a joy it was to just speak forth the way to heaven! After a blessed time of making the gospel known in as many kraals as possible, we had to return to school, catching the bus at the same milk station.

While we waited near the road, people passing through the bush would look incredibly – then stop, come over, and swarm around at the bus stop. How they listened to each word spoken. Even a witch doctor, with three inflated goat gall bladders suspended from her hair at the back of her head, listened thoughtfully. What a privilege it was to be there as an ambassador of the King of Kings, delivering His message of eternal life – the way to heaven, to be with Him forever. Isaiah 43 says, "... Thus saith the Lord, your redeemer ... I will even make a way in the wilderness ... This people have I formed for myself; they shall shew forth my praise ...". The bus arrived. Someone on it called out to the people, "They will lead you astray!" He had come from Johannesburg, where they came in contact with Communists. One who had come with us from the kraal looked up, and boldly answered with truths from the Lord.

This bus was fine, for it was a government mail bus. We reached Gollel, and stayed overnight with the family of the African preacher. He told us people would be coming for a service. He set a flat bottle on its broad side. With its own wax, he adhered our burning candle to the bottle. Soon the people gathered, and what a joy it was to worship the Lord with them. A demon-possessed boy, who had been running and running over the mountains, came in and listened quietly to God's word.

At 4 a.m., we made our way through the tall grass over to the makeshift "road." We wondered if the second bus was repaired yet. Eventually, headlights appeared. We waved our flashlight up and down with long strokes, as we had been kindly instructed to do, so the driver would see we needed a ride. No, it was not the bus, but it was the long, flat-bottomed truck to take its place, all right! We climbed on – Ida in the back, and I in the front. What a joy! The repaired gears shifted normally now!

But another defect surfaced. The steering wheel would not turn left! This considerably slowed our progress when the road curved left. There were no tunnels. The road followed the line of least resistance around the mountains. It was amazing how often the road curved to the left. To follow it, the driver went a short distance on the curve, turned the steering wheel to the right as far as it would go, backed the bus as far as possible, and then went forward, thus inching his way to the top of the mountain – somewhat later in the day.

Approaching one mountain, we saw the road turned to the left at a 90-degree angle. There were no fences, as herdboys watched the cattle. Stretched out at the foot of the mountain, on the right, was a large, flat, grassy area with no bushes – just the right space so a long truck could turn around in a circle. A driver has many things to think of, and cannot always see extra scenery at the side. The Lord gave me wisdom to suggest making a big circle to the right in that space, and thus be headed straight up

*Bus road back to Mhlosheni (at right). It leads to
Beersheeba in front of Christine Trevvett (at left).*

the mountain road. The driver circled to the right. The Lord helped the truck to climb quite a ways up – before the driver had to resort to his inching technique to follow the left-curving road. When we descended that mountain onto the plain, a child the driver's assistant knew came running from a kraal. Through the window, the child handed over a whole chicken they had apparently boiled in its entirety, in one of their black pots. The assistant enjoyed his meal immensely, and generously shared it, too!

We were making good progress, when suddenly, the truck stopped, as the engine died and could not be revived. We were on a slope, and easily rolled out of the road onto the shoulder. We got off and walked over to the grassy bank beside the road. The driver, once again, placed his money box on my lap, and hurriedly crawled under the truck with his assistant, to get the motor going.

They were under the cab for some hours. This was a blessing, as it gave opportunity to visit with the passengers one by one, and tell them about the Saviour. It was a perfect example of Romans 8:28 – "And we know that all things work together for good to them that love God ...". At last, the driver climbed into the cab, and the engine sputtered to a start. At the welcome sound, all reboarded, and before long, reached the place where Ida and I had to disembark. This last truck trip of nearly sixty miles took about twelve hours.

We happily walked the rest of the way home, thanking the Lord for the fruitful journey in which He had brought some to Himself. Jesus said, "... with God all things are possible" (Matthew 19:26).

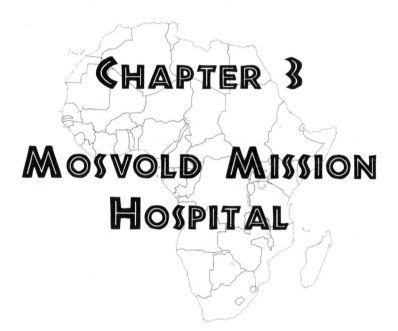

Chapter 3

Mosvold Mission Hospital

Schools closed, and our annual missionary Bible conference was held near the coast. We girls slept on cots in a large dormitory. It was such a grand reunion that happy visiting continued far into the night. After the conference, I was to drive Oddweig Thompson 300 miles north to her Swaziland mission station. It was difficult to get enough sleep (even with a blanket-covered head), because of the excited dormitory chatter. But the Lord helped me to take Oddweig to her home, and then return to my station.

Then Jeanette Eckel, a teacher from California, two young Swazi girls, and I went by bus to take the gospel to mothers and children in northern Swaziland. The Swazi men were away, working in Johannesburg gold mines.

We reached the kraal where we were to stay. On Saturday, the children's meetings would commence. The people had no clocks, so it was interesting to see how they would know what time to come! Friday night, the kraal grandmother announced, "Tomorrow at the time when the sun gets warm, the herdboys will take the cattle to a place and leave them, come to the meeting, and then go back and fetch them later." The Lord helped three children to receive Him.

As the week progressed, my breathing became difficult. I coughed continually, and had to sit up at night to breathe. Knowing this made it extremely difficult, if not impossible, for the other three in the hut to get any sleep, I said, "I can go out on the mountain to sleep!" I was so thankful when they said, "No." It was winter. It was desperately cold out on the mountain. It gave a wonderful realization of a little of what the Lord suffered for us. Luke 21:37 says, "And in the day time he was teaching in the temple; and at night he went out, and abode in the mount …". Jesus said, "… Foxes have holes, and birds of the air have nests; but the Son of man hath not where to lay his head" (Luke 9:58). He, Who created the whole world, had no place to lay His head.

We did not know I had double pneumonia. But as soon as the day a bus came heading back to our mission school, we set out early to catch it. There was a strange, ethereal, floating feeling, trying to climb the hills along the way.

The Lord helped us get there in time. The bus bumped over the road, and finally, reached Gollel. We spent the night with the African preacher's family.

At 4 a.m., we set out for the road again. We heard the other bus coming, and waved our flashlight up and down in the darkness. The driver brought the bus to a halt. The bus had no door. They seated us in the front. Bitter, cold air came flying through the doorway as we rode along. It was a blessing when the bus stopped for passengers, and the frigid stream of air ceased.

Some Swazis got on, with their semi-circular sickles draped over their heads – the sharp edges resting on their hair! They balanced the wobbling sickles with unbelievable precision. (In school, girls run races with pop bottles on top of their round

ETTC girls balancing and carrying firewood.

heads.) They are used to balancing heavy pots of water. They set leaves on top to keep the water from sloshing out, as their feet walk on the potholed ground. They carry hoes the same way – balancing the long handles in the middle.

A witch doctor got on, with the typical three inflated goat gall bladders hanging down the back of her hair. Weak with

Nurse Gininda (L) and Elsa Swalheim at MMH.

fever, I could not speak, but handed her a tract telling the way to heaven. She could not read, but took it, knowing a child could read it to her. When we reached the mission school, I told the nurse I was not feeling well. I did not realize it, but she immediately phoned our mission hospital in the Ubombo Mountains. Lydia Rogalsky, one of the missionaries, had a car. Lydia kindly took me to Mosvold Mission Hospital (MMH).

When we got up there, two folks – one on either side – helped me walk to the X-ray machine. Dr. Morrill, from Oregon, came.

MMH gospel team.

He had originally planned to be a veterinarian. But he received Christ as his Saviour, and then became a medical doctor. He and his family of seven were going to China. But that door closed.

It felt so good to rest from climbing the hills. The doctor and nurses were all in white, so the thought came that the Lord might take me home to heaven. How wonderful that would be! But right away, Psalm 118:17 came to mind: "I shall not die, but live, and declare the works of the Lord."

Dr. Morrill said lungs resemble a bunch of grapes. They were filling up with fluid. He said to breathe as deeply as possible each hour. That was painful. But I was glad to follow his good

Tongaland girls at MMH.

Zululand children.

directions, being so thankful to have a doctor. In some places, there was only one doctor for 100,000 people!

I coughed the excess fluid into a tin cup. My lips formed sores, which failed to heal. The doctor asked what was being put on them. "Vaseline," I responded. He immediately said to use lanolin, instead. My lips began to heal right away. As the days passed, the breathing exercises became easier; the fever subsided, and I felt stronger.

A specialist came from Durban to check the tuberculosis patients. He was shown my chest X-rays, and could not believe they were the same lungs shown in X-rays ten days before. The Lord had marvelously healed them.

It was good to "lie down in green pastures." The Lord leads us "beside the still waters," when we need to be there. We may have a longing to go to heaven, but if He still has work He wants us to do on earth, He restores our souls (Psalm 23).

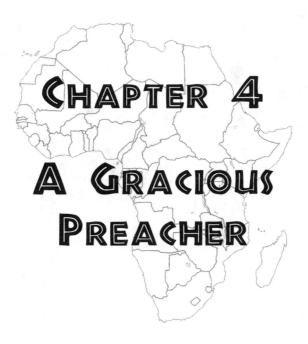

CHAPTER 4

A GRACIOUS PREACHER

Galatians 6:1 says, "Brethren, if a man be overtaken in a fault, ye which are spiritual, restore such an one in the spirit of meekness …". We want to do this lovingly. Proverbs 9:8 says, "… rebuke a wise man, and he will love thee." Matthew

Herdboys' Sunday School on far mountain.

Ida in stream at first mountain to the herdboys' Sunday School.

5:9 says, "Blessed are the peacemakers …". This does bring wonderful blessing.

One of the preachers stopped attending the preachers' quarterly meetings. This discouraged the other preachers. The missionaries began to speak of it. This was wrong, as the Bible says, "Speak not evil one of another, brethren …" (James 4:11). The loving way of the Lord would be to "… go and tell him his fault between thee

Herdboys coming to Sunday School. Center boy carries bush knife. Mhlosheni in background.

and him alone …" (Matthew 18:15). The Lord helped to make a list of verses like "Not forsaking the assembling of ourselves together …" (Hebrews 10:25) and Jesus said, "… If a man love me, he will keep my words …" (John 14:23).

I took Ida, the orphan child, and walked over to the preacher's kraal. The Lord wonderfully provided an opportunity to have an encouraging visit with the preacher, while Ida climbed trees with other children there.

I first asked if it would be all right for us to continue Sunday School classes for the little cattle herders three mountains away during vacation, when the regular Sunday School was closed. (The herders could not attend Sunday

Some of the herdboys' Sunday School teachers.

School in the church, because they had to keep their cattle out of neighbors' fields.) The preacher was delighted, saying, "School closes, but not the Lord's school!" He was deeply appreciative, as always, because Isaiah 52:7 says, "How beautiful upon the mountains are the feet of him that bringeth good tidings ... that publisheth salvation ...". When he saw students returning from

Large, white school chapel (in center).

having Sunday School classes for little herders near their cattle, he would encouragingly call out to us, "Hello, Beautiful Feet!" The Lord helped to lovingly mention the helpful Bible verses, and Ida and I returned home.

Time passed. The time came for the quarterly meeting. I praised the Lord – word came our preacher was there! When he came home, he reported in our school chapel (as he always did when he had been to a meeting for the Lord's work). He nearly wept, as he told

FCHS Home Economics teacher

of the wonderful reconciliation the Lord helped the leaders to have. He said, "God has His nurses who bind up the wounds." I "... thanked God, and took courage" (Acts 28:15).

FCHS classroom.

FCHS juniors: (L-R) Samuel, teacher, Abner, Alfred, Ablon, Samuel, Lucy, Agrippa, Thomas, Elijah and Simeon

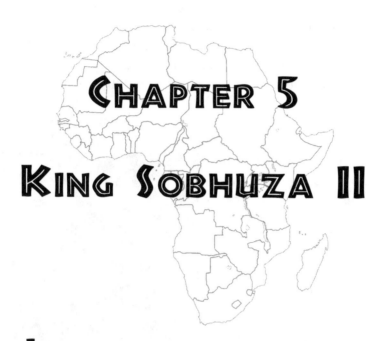

CHAPTER 5

KING SOBHUZA II

In 1963, King Sobhuza II, of Swaziland, was the longest reigning monarch in the world, at that time. They called him "The Lion of the Swazis." His mother was very fond of Franson Christian High School (FCHS), our Mhlosheni Mission School (where I taught for twelve years). Malla Moe, a missionary from Norway, had visited the king's mother and led her to the Lord. Malla was so well known, she actually received a letter simply addressed to "Malla Moe, Africa." Africa is so vast that it is three times larger than the United States.

Sobhuza was to be honored at our school on a periodic government visit in 1950. He asked if Malla Moe could be there that day. When Malla entered the room where the king and his counsellors were drinking tea, she was touched as Sobhuza stood courteously to greet her. She said she had visited with his mother many times, and that his mother died saved. Sobhuza said he remembered. He said Malla loved his mother, and his mother loved Malla. Malla urged Sobhuza to become a Christian, too – so he could meet his mother in heaven. She later wrote

Subhuza a letter, saying it would be wonderful to have a king in Swaziland who loved God. She included a picture of his mother and herself. He wrote, thanking Malla for the picture, but said nothing about meeting his mother in heaven.

It was customary for missionaries to tell the king goodbye when leaving his country. Before Wilfred and Ruth Hart left on furlough, Wilfred took Sobhuza a present. A go-between presents the gift; so Jonah, a Swazi preacher, went with him. Two World Health Organization officials were speaking with the king. They continued staying – far beyond their appointed time. Finally, the king looked at Wilfred and said, "Masikhulume ngolimi lwethu." ("Let's talk in our language.") Wilfred knew five languages. He grew up conversing with herdboys on his white parents' farm. The WHO officials departed. Jonah stepped in front of Sobhuza and fumbled nervously in his excitement

Jonah.

– trying to open the package. "Give me my Bible!" said the king happily – taking it half-unwrapped.

One day, King Sobhuza invited our school to come to his summer "palace" out in the bush country. I was going on furlough soon, so I wrote this letter to Sobhuza:

Franson Christian High School
Mhlosheni, Swaziland
October 4, 1963

Lion, (That was the way the Swazis always addressed him.)

I greet you in the name of the Lord Jesus Christ, Who died for us on the cross, with Proverbs 14:34 – "Righteousness

FCHS. Road on right leads to Antioch, Jerusalem and Jericho.

exalteth a nation: but sin is a reproach to any people." We trust we of Mhlosheni will visit you at your home Saturday; but I do not know whether I can get an opportunity to speak with you, so I will write you this letter. I will say goodbye, since at the end of the year I will return overseas to my home there a little while, the Lord willing. I am thanking God, because He enabled me to be here in Swaziland these past six years, and to read the Bible with many people here in your country. I was happy to hear from the Harts (after they were there with you to say goodbye) that you love the word of God and to talk about verses in it.

In visiting Swazi kraals, we came to one place where there was a witch doctor. She was not only a witch doctor, but she taught others to be witch doctors, too. We read in Deuteronomy 18:10–13 and Revelation 21:8 (and the verses were written out in the letter), *"There shall not be found among you ... a witch ...".* I spoke with that witch doctor about leaving this *work of darkness, because consulting with ancestral spirits is an abomination to God* (their word for God is 'UNkulunkulu' – 'The Great, Great One')*; and people who are abominable shall have their part in the lake of fire. She said that you said some of* *the money she earns from this work must be sent to you. Since you are one of those who fear God Who is Almighty, I hope this witch doctor did not understand well; also that you will want to explain better for those who are accustomed to meet at Lobamba* (the king's ruling palace) *about that occupation – so that they will stop it in order that the Swazi nation may be blessed. Thank you. They can be thankful, too – to be enlightened. There were sick ones who sought the witch doctor only. They say they speak to the ancestors' departed spirits, but the spirits do not answer them. One of the Christians said the departed spirits are not God. It is not right to worship them, because God said, "I am the Lord thy God ... thou shalt have no other gods before me" (Exodus 20:2, 3). They say that occupation doesn't help any! They are still sick. Now they are sickened by it, too.*

May the Lord help you to correct those who are like that ... .

When our school reached the summer palace, a cow was being caught to make a feast. The teachers were invited to tea. The king came in, barefoot, dressed in a large square of bright, colorful, cotton material tied on at his right shoulder and his right side. He sat down with tremendous poise – with the serene composure of an American Indian!

One of our junior college students, who came with us, brought a cup of tea to each one of us. But Sobhuza never touched his. (Kings dare not drink, for fear of being poisoned – unless the king's own taster, whom he knows well, tastes it first.) He sat there, absolutely at ease – as though he were drinking, just like the rest of us.

We spoke of the long, cement ditch above our school, leading down around the mountain from a spring. Water from the spring provided electricity in the evenings. Other things were discussed. Suddenly, the king rose and said he must now go to his council meeting, which was always held at night. I thought, "Oh, dear! We have not spoken of heaven yet!"

Sobhuza went around the circle, briefly shaking hands with each standing person. As his bare feet finally stood in front of me, I praised the Lord He helped to say what a joy it was to be in Swaziland. I was so thankful he still stood there listening – to hear the Bible says God hath <u>given</u> to us eternal life, and this life is in His Son. He that hath the Son hath life. "It is a <u>wonderful</u> gift!" exclaimed the king, and then hurried on to his meeting. Maybe the Lord helped him to receive that gift before he died. His son – when he became king – had Christian songs sung at a gathering.

There was only one time in Africa that I thought of leaving and returning to stay in America. But the Lord sent an unusual happiness, which overcame that day's discouragement. I was in the office in the grade school building at Mhlosheni, where I sold Bibles, hymnbooks, slates, slate pencils and other school supplies at recess time. It was the close of a hot day. The office door was open wide. Classes ended for the day. As the children

In lower left, grade school is at right of the two high school buildings.

streamed past in the hall, one little girl stepped into the doorway and said, "Ngiyakuthanda" (I love you), "Nkosazana."

I had never seen that child before, and never saw her again. It was as though the Lord had sent an angel – encouraging me to be "stedfast, unmoveable, always abounding in the work of the

Lord, forasmuch as ye know that your labour is not in vain in the Lord" (1 Corinthians 15:58).

The Lord worked miracles to encourage the Christians in the difficult, early days of evangelism. Johane Gamede was one of Malla Moe's faithful helpers with the Gospel Wagon mission work. They would leave Bethel Mission Station and reach Zulus down in the bush country, where the vegetation was so dense, it was easy to get lost. They marked the trees to be able to find their way back out. To find a kraal, they listened for a rooster to crow. They went in that direction – and there found people.

Johane could not learn to read. One day, he went up on a mountain to pray. He came down in the evening, picked up a Zulu Bible – and read!

Moses and Aaron, two sons of a powerful Zulu chief, heard the gospel in the army and became Christians. When they returned home, they faithfully proclaimed the gospel. More Zulus became Christians. They sent word, asking Johane to come and baptize them. When Johane arrived, the Zulu chief sent his warriors against the Christian group. Moses, the older converted son, rushed forth to stop them. Moses was next in line to become chief (though he became an evangelist instead), so the warriors had to obey him. But one spear had already pierced Johane's thigh. Johane somehow managed to get down the mountain. (Inga Brunvaer and Evelyn Sodren, two of the missionaries, said the mountain was so steep they could only get up by holding onto their horse's tail.) Johane lay there at the foot of the mountain for three days. The Lord healed the wound, but the injury was so severe that Johane always had to use a cane after that.

Fredrik Franson, the Norwegian evangelist who founded the mission now known as The Evangelical Alliance Mission, never married. He visited missionaries throughout the world to encourage them, so he was frugal – putting his treasure up in heaven. He carried all his earthly possessions in one satchel. He had three socks. He could wash one, while wearing the others. When asked why he always rode in third class on trains, he said it was because there was no fourth. He reached South Africa and visited Johane.

Some time later, it was so hot one night that Johane got up and walked outdoors in the cooler air. Suddenly, he saw in the sky Fredrick Franson, who looked down and said to him, "You go so slowly down there!" Then Franson receded into an open door, where there was a very bright light.

When mail reached South Africa from America, a month or so later, it confirmed that that was the very time Franson had gone to be with the Lord. Johane was so touched that he went all over the mountains preaching the gospel.

Years later, I met Johane at Bethel, and told him I was so encouraged to hear he had preached so diligently, after he saw Fredrik Franson go to heaven. "He went right up there!" Johane said excitedly, pointing with his cane to a certain place in the sky.

Johane Gamede resting at Bethel.

Chapter 6

Jonathan's Kraal

There was a boy in Swaziland whose name was Dog. He had often been at Bethel Mission Station, where he heard the gospel. Malla Moe, who was the missionary there, was going on furlough. On the way to the coast, she and the Swazi Christians accompanying her reached "The Place of Power" – where they spent the night. Before they resumed their journey the next morning, Dog overtook them. He had left home at 3 a.m. to reach them in time. Malla was the first one he had heard the gospel from. She often said Dog should be saved – and get a new name. That morning, he received the Saviour. Dog was renamed "Jonathan." He became an evangelist. He was chaplain for the African forces during World War II. When he returned home and gathered his family together for family devotions, they often sang a hymn the troops had sung.

When our school vacation time came, students who lived in hostels (dormitories) went home. Some walked twenty-five miles. It was a joy to go with Betty and Saraphina, two older Christian Swazi girls, to have a week of children's Bible classes at the kraal where Jonathan and his family lived.

The sun seemed to be quickly dropping down to the time "when the people look beautiful" (which is what the people call sunset). Betty, Saraphina, and I bade farewell to the missionary who had brought us as far as her vehicle could safely go. The crude mountain road was quite passable at one time, but now, it began to disappear down its several gullies during each rain. Starting the hour's walk to our destination, we descended, and fended – for ourselves. We could easily see Jonathan's kraal at the top of the next mountain. The gullies increased in number and magnitude, as we approached the slowly moving stream separating the two mountains.

There was no grass in the soil there at all, as we approached the water. Saraphina was carrying our water jug on her head. "Oh, I'm sorry!" she called out, as the cork of the jug bounced off and rolled down the dark, red creek bank towards the running water. She had tried to adjust the large jug, as she minced her way down the bank which sloped sharply to the right. While she brought the jug down, I retrieved the cork and tried to clean it. The cork's wet sides were covered with red dust. "That's all right!" I said, gratefully remembering some Kleenex my sister had sent. A piece of the tissue soon surrounded most of the cork. The jug resumed its high position, and we continued on our journey.

The bank before us was steeper, but not slanting – so we made our way up quite easily. As we climbed towards our home for the next eight days, we could see that Jonathan Shongwe and his family were doing what they could to discourage the soil's disappearance. Healthy looking cactus plants were growing in the middle of the gulley we were passing.

As we approached the kraal, Betty suddenly said, "Here comes the preacher!" Barefooted Jonathan was coming around the cattle kraal noiselessly, and smiling broadly. We already felt at home. He led us into our room in a spacious three-room house. A common ceiling of grass lay on horizontal poles some distance above where the tops of the rooms' dividing walls ended.

Two large, neatly rolled and tied grass mats hung from the horizontal poles above our room. Two strange, wooden structures hung there, too. They were yokes for oxen.

During a hailstorm, one can think more easily under a grass roof than under a corrugated iron one. But a thunderstorm is

Dome shaped hut.

not too pleasant for an African. Often, his grass home is shaped like a low dome. Lightning can set his home on fire. How can he escape, especially if the lightning strikes while he is sleeping?

The family gathered for supper before the first evening service. The chicken, gravy and thick corn porridge were delicious.

The first bell for the service had been rung earlier, so the people would have time to walk from the surrounding mountains' kraals.

When we entered the church, the people were singing – as

Framework for new grass hut.

Moving framework upside down to a new location.

they often do before a service. We were given places on a side bench at the front of the church. The rest of the family found places – womenfolk on the left and menfolk on the right. Finally, Jonathan himself approached the chair behind the table at the front and knelt to pray.

There was a candle in the middle of the wooden table. A kerosene lamp hung farther down in the center of the long building. There were three dim windows on each side. We could only see dark silhouettes of the people sitting on the rows of backless benches, extending to the back wall of the building. Most of the men were shrouded in dark blankets – an attire quite different from that worn during the day. The evenings were chilly, even though we were in the lower bushveld.

Jonathan was wearing an overcoat, though his feet were bare. Probably the overcoat was one he had had when serving with the army for Britain. Then we had a feast from God's word, which was better than our necessary food (Job 23:12).

As we made our way back from the meeting, we could hear the people singing as they traveled over the mountains to their kraals. I thought of Jonathan's words when he had said there was one here who had left parents at home, and come across the sea with its dangers – "For," he said, "have not many disappeared in the sea? But this one has come to us. Why? For the sake of the gospel!" But the dangers seemed to really be before <u>these</u> people, as they groped their various ways through the thick darkness; for there was no starlight present that night. And I wished my parents he had mentioned, had been there to see the <u>gratitude</u> in the hearts of those who had come out of darkness into the marvelous light of the gospel.

I asked the girls the name of the huge kraal dog. "What shall I do if I ever meet him in the darkness – just speak his name?" I asked. He would do no harm, they explained. I asked, "How do you know?" They said, "Because he has been taught to know Christians. He will never bite them. He never does when they come to the kraal." I asked, "How can that be?" They answered, "He has been taught." I was glad he had been, when in the middle of the night I heard his voice, which was in direct proportion to his size.

It was a delight to unroll the bedroll, which had remained quite dustproof inside two large, plastic buttermilk bags. We had brought two heavy drapes for warmth. An afghan was not brought, lest it might become inhabited.

"What's that?" asked Betty with alarm, looking at our window. There was a long, snaky object hanging down the side of the window. It proved to be only a cowhide thong, used to

Kraal on a mountainside.

hold up the window. The top window would not go up all the way. There was one pane out, which probably made the draft which caused a cold (which disappeared quickly).

The kraal was swept nicely with branches from bushes. The people wisely carried branches, like umbrellas, for protection from the sun.

Jonathan showed us where different kraals were. His kraal was located up on a knoll, and we could see all around. "You seem to know everyone!" I said. "They are our people!" he exclaimed, smiling. He asked if I had come from Norway. He warned us there were fierce dogs at some kraals, so we took some leaves from certain shrubs along the way. The girls said dogs did not bite you if you entered a kraal carrying these leaves. I asked, "Why not?" The girls responded, "It's just the custom." Perhaps people carried them to show they came peaceably, and dogs knew that sign. But we were glad a herdboy was going with us to the second kraal when a dog bounded out, and the boy had to beat him back. I squeezed my leaves hard – as unobtrusively as possible – hoping a man sitting there (making sharp posts on slim poles with a machete) would not notice, in case he would be offended that we were afraid of his dogs. He spoke politely, then continued his occupation.

"Would you like to receive Jesus?" one asked him after some conversation. "I am still thinking," the man said.

Others in the family were called. The boy we had met on the way came with us as we entered an unusually large, grass hut. The floor was hard and clean. Everything was in place. The grandmother joined us. A young man entered who talked much. When asked if he attended the church, he said, "No." Hebrews 10:25 was read: "Not forsaking the assembling of ourselves together as the manner of some is ...". Verses from Matthew 24 were also read. The man who was "still thinking" was <u>listening</u> so, as he heard Jesus is coming again – suddenly – at a time when people are not expecting Him; even as the people in the time of Noah "knew not until the flood came, and took them all away ... Therefore be ye also ready: for in such an hour as ye think not the Son of man cometh." Those who have not received Christ as their Saviour cannot go to heaven. For "whosoever was not found written in the book of life was cast into the lake of fire" (Revelation 20:15). It was so good to tell people the truth, so they could escape hell and have joy forever. We said, "Jesus might even come today," and explained how dangerous it is to wait, and neglect salvation. Saraphina often mentioned this solemn truth in her lessons with the children. The Lord helped twelve children to receive Him. One of them, Maria, asked us to pray for her, because she was going to tell her father about something wrong she had done. Saraphina said her father drank beer, and would probably beat the girl.

The man (who was Jonathan's brother) came with us to the edge of the kraal to show us the next path to take. The words of the Bible are quick and powerful. We said, "We hope to see you at church!" And he came! He sat in the back in his tight, red skirt, listening intently. The people said, "He wants to believe." Others say they want to believe, but say they are bound by sin. It is wonderful Jesus can set the prisoners free from Satan's chains.

"Boy," who was saved in the children's meetings, was going to attend our school the next year. He and his mother lived with the Shongwes, as his father had died. His mother was Jonathan's sister – and such a dear lady. That evening, she and Mrs. Shongwe were going down the mountainside past the cattle kraal, to the wide stretch of cactus plants, which served as a windbreak. I joined them and told them about those we had talked with in the kraals that day. They knew those people well. Jonathan's sister said, "And you left your mother and father and came clear here to Africa!" And they were marveling, because they were thinking it was hard, so I mentioned how Jesus left heaven for us! "And all His glory that He had!" added the sister. "And He died for us!" said Mrs. Shongwe. It was such a joy to hear them. It is wonderful when people understand what the Lord has done for us and are thankful. It was marvelous how they spontaneously thought of the salvation Christ has provided!

They said, "We're so glad you've come to talk with the children. They come to school – but they need Jesus."

The people ate cactus plant buds. They said they were very sweet.

They washed their feet with a stone. It rubbed off the hard, scaly skin formed on the bottom and sides of their bare feet. Cracks were very deep in the rough skin, but the people did not say anything. So perhaps the cracks caused no pain. They were very patient people. They made knives very sharp by whetting them with stones. Toenails were trimmed with a nice, sharp pocketknife.

Betty taught a children's lesson using two stories I had written out in Zulu. She had used them at another Sunday School in Zululand. Swazis understood Zulu very well. At that time, Swazis used the Zulu Bible, as there was no Swazi Bible in print. The noontime church services sometimes lasted for three hours.

Africans speak with amazing proverbs, which mean much to them. The proverbs are similar to those we know – such as "Don't count your chickens before they hatch." I had not been in South Africa long enough to learn the language well. So when Saraphina asked if I would be taking the next children's lesson, I mentioned that she could do it so much better. Surprised, Saraphina asked, "Don't you love Jesus?" Africans speak simply – just what they are thinking – like children. This was very helpful to me, and I quickly set to work on the lesson, with the Lord wonderfully helping.

It has been said that Africans think we are like children. An African lies down at night on a hard floor, with a wooden pillow under his head, and sleeps soundly. Only spoiled or sick children roll and toss on the floor, until given a soft skin and wad of downy feathers. Men eat when the sun is up. Only children have to be fed in the early morning. Men run long distances without tiring. They can kill a snake with the first blow, and slay an animal with the first spear thrust. One who cannot do these things is only a "boy."

We may think Africans are black and pug-nosed. They think we look washed out, colorless and pointed-nosed.

They think we cannot remember. They can recall what we said, when we think we did not say it. If we cannot remember, they can tell us where we were, who was with us, in what month it was, where the sun was in the sky, how big the leaves were on the trees, who passed by when we were talking, what others said, and they can quote us word for word.

They may not notice a picture hanging crooked on the wall, but the very first time a man walks across a room, they can describe his disposition and dramatize his peculiarity of walk.

Swazis have a custom of carrying sticks as they travel. One young man had his good-sized one anchored in the top buttonhole of his coat, after one of the evening services.

One evening, there was a rustling in one of the orange trees. They said something about a snake. One boy threw a heavy stick just where the leaves had been moving, but it was not a snake. Chickens roosted in the trees.

It was unusual to have orange trees at a kraal – and quite refreshing. "Boy" handed me his pocketknife. It cut an orange easily into sections. It was handy to use, as our hands were not always clean. The people sheared the goats' hair a little with a pocketknife to remove cockleburs.

They used an iron bar about four feet long for digging sweet potatoes. One boy used the ashes from the fire to wash a water bucket. Another boy ate a raw sweet potato, though more often, they set them by the fire, and ate them after they were baked.

The morning we butchered a chicken, its cleaned-out digestive system was soon being roasted on a piece of wood in the fire. Nothing was wasted. A herdboy had the skinned head of a goat that was butchered. He was probably going to boil the head in a three-legged pot.

A man came to visit. His sandals were made by hand from a tire. The thick soles would wear for a long time.

Long, black soot "stalactites" hung from the grass roof of the cooking hut. A sudden fluttering in one dark corner revealed a chicken (bound for dinner), with string or grass tied around its legs. It was changing its position.

The children enjoyed playing Simon Says "Hands up" and "Hands down" – trying to find a coin hidden under someone's hand. To make music, they pulled together two tines of a fork. They also played games with kernels of corn.

Betty said sometimes the children came running to announce a missionary went by on the road. When asked, "How do you know?" they said, "Because she was smiling!" The Boers do not smile as a rule.

One night, a heathen girl and her baby stayed at the kraal. I was preparing Zulu Romans Bible study lessons, and had read so much to the children before meetings, while waiting for more to arrive, that my voice was fading away. So Mrs. Shongwe read to us. First, she sent a child to fetch her glasses. She started with the first chapter of Romans. How she did drink in the words herself! "Paul is writing," said Mrs. Shongwe. "To whom? – 'I am debtor both to the Greeks, and to the Barbarians; both to the wise, and to the unwise.' What does debtor mean? Paul had found Jesus as his Saviour. He was so thankful that he wanted everyone else to know Him, too, and he felt it was his responsibility to tell them. He was so happy in his heart now, and he wanted all the other people to come to Jesus, so they could have everlasting life, too. Yes! Yes!" she said, and continued, "Because that, when they knew God, they glorified him not as God, neither were thankful; but became vain in their imaginations, and their foolish heart was darkened. Professing themselves to be wise, they became fools, And changed the glory of the uncorruptible God into an image made like to corruptible man, and … changed the truth of God into a lie, and worshipped and served the creature more than the Creator, who is blessed for ever. Amen." Every once in a while, as she was reading, she nodded her head, saying, "It's just like that!" It was so good the heathen girl was there, listening.

I helped make cracked corn, called "stamp," in a large, halfway-hollowed-out tree stump. We put whole kernels of corn in the stump. Then two people – each with a pole like that used to tamp in a fence post – stood opposite each other and took turns pounding the corn. Water was added, so the corn was not ground to a powder. When it was stamped long enough, we spread it out to dry in a wide, round basket made of grass. We also ground corn for porridge. The grinder had a very large cranking wheel on one side, and a smaller one on the other side. Two people stood and cranked with pieces of wood put into the manufactured holes. It was easier than grinding with stones, though the people often used two nice grinding stones.

The children in Jonathan's household had learned Psalm 23. Someone had taken my classes at school, so I could come early with Betty and Saraphina. Two days later, Alfred, Siphiwe, Ivy and Gilbert arrived, after walking the long journey home from our school. When they reached our kraal, the family all gathered in the dining room (the largest of the three rooms in the house). Jonathan read Bible verses and prayed, thanking God for keeping them safe while they were away. And we sang a hymn.

Kind hands brought tea to our room each morning, which we enjoyed with cookies that other kind hands had sent along with us. Breakfast usually consisted of corn porridge or corn porridge cooked with pumpkin, which we happily ate together at 10 or 11 a.m. – followed by tea. They raised only white corn, as they felt yellow corn was difficult to digest. The white corn had short ears with large, round, white kernels. Pumpkin mixed in with the porridge made it bright yellow. It tasted so good. The people drank sour milk, as there was no way to keep milk fresh. One dinner was thick, sour milk, tea, bread and jam. The boys said when they milked a cow the cream came last, but there was probably not enough to make butter.

At night, they took a lighted piece of stiff grass, lifted the cooking pot's lid, and put the lighted grass under the lid to see how the porridge was cooking. It was too dark to see inside otherwise, because the cooking pot hid the light of the fire.

For one supper, our plates were heaped full of tiny, round,

green beans with white scars – grown chiefly in Swaziland. For another supper, we had stamp and three kinds of beans. All were very, very good. We often had sweet potatoes. We had partially clabbered sour milk with raw ground white corn or raw ground brown corn. To avoid tuberculosis, I did not eat much clabbered sour milk, and took tea and porridge without milk, too – which was easy, as some of them did the same.

If we had meat, most of the time it was chicken. To scald a chicken before dressing it, they poured boiling water over it from an iron teakettle. One day, they butchered a goat. That night, we had the duodenum and subsequent parts. I started in bravely, after having learned from previous experience that at least the contents were removed. But after encountering several stones, I decided I had had enough – much to Jonathan's delight, I believe, because he finished it with gusto (though they are quite happy to know we will eat their food). I discovered with the first bite that the other piece of "meat" from the goat that night was a strip of thickish skin. I tried to concentrate on how delicious chicken skin was (before cholesterol was learned of), but the stiff hairs caused the prohibition of that sensation, and Jonathan had all the rest to add to his nice Thanksgiving dinner.

At times, I would read from the Bible about Daniel, Joseph or David. Soon, a cluster of children gathered around to listen. Sometimes, children arrived early at the church before a meeting, so they came running to hear a story. They were from kraals farther away, so I told them how to be <u>saved</u>, too. I asked one little boy if he knew the way to heaven. "Qhake!" (Not at all!) he replied. When asked whether he knew Jesus died for us, he said, "Qhake!" I could tell he was one of the new children.

We pinned a yellow cotton strip on each child. We wrote each one's name on a white paper and stuck it on the yellow strip. Each day they came, we stuck on a square of blue tape. If one brought another child, we put a red one on, too. They were very eager to earn red ones. Some children were just brought from the wild. Two had rather long hair. How they would look at the other children, and try to keep up with the motions for the choruses. They would look at me often, too, as though I were strange. It was so good to see them drinking in the Bible messages.

Sometimes, children became sleepy in the evening meeting. To avoid falling off the wooden benches, they would just lean straight forward, with their chests on their knees. Some of their names were Green, General Gamede, Short Noonday Meal, Crocodile, and This Sickness (whose mother was probably ill when the child was born).

Jonathan was going to ride his white horse, Sweet, to attend the preachers' meeting at Bethel. That night, before his journey, there was stamping and stamping outdoors. It looked like swaying warriors were surrounding our huts. It was difficult to see in the darkness, but they did not seem to have spears. In the house, where beans were stored, a light appeared – and then vanished. The stampers stayed in a solid line, and did not come any closer. It seemed they might be waiting for Jonathan to come out. They were still stamping at 6 a.m. It was still too dark to see them clearly.

Then I heard Jonathan praying. He and his wife always prayed early in the mornings. He was praying to the Lord about leaving us in His hands. I wondered if the warriors knew he was going away, and they were going to come against us – and this was just the prelude. But I was happy and quite at rest, realizing that all things work together for good to us. Even if my life needed to be taken to bring souls to the Lord, it would be a joy to go to be with Him, and thus enable others to be with Him – if that were the only way their hearts might be touched.

When at last dawn arrived, large holes became visible which had been formed in the ground by stamping feet. And those who had seemed to be warriors – were actually children who had gotten up early to stamp on beans to shell them, before the sun got too hot!

We sat around the campfire where peanuts were roasting – in the remains of a once three-legged (but now two-legged) pot. The shelled peanuts were poured onto a saucer-like structure with irregularly broken sides. The pot was propped up on its legless side against an iron. They poured on saltwater – making the nuts delicious.

There was a welcome piece of tree trunk, just the right size for a seat, near the cooking hut. I often sat on it, and one morning was going to pick it up to move it closer to Mrs. Shongwe – only to find it was a tree stump, well rooted in the earth!

A cattle kraal.

The Lord helps herdboys to be expert marksmen. They grow up practicing accuracy with the splendid weapons they make. One day, I was passing by the cattle kraal. An ox came out, began to snort, and approach. In a flash, a herdboy threw his huge knobkerrie (a short, wooden club with a knob on one end), crashing it onto the startled ox – stopping the animal in its tracks – preventing its forward lunge. "… God … is a shield unto them that put their trust in him" (Proverbs 30:5).

At one mission station, a snake was discovered sailing around on the top of the water in a very large, rectangular underground storage tank. The tank's width, as well as its length, could be measured in yards. A herdboy rushed up with his slingshot and killed the racing snake with one stone. "… the Lord is … my deliverer … in him will I trust …" (2 Samuel 22:2–3).

We praise the Lord not one of our missionaries in South Africa has been killed by a poisonous snake!

CHAPTER 7

THE PLACE FAR OUT

During one vacation, it was possible to go to Esinceni Mission Station, en route to Empumakude (The Place Far Out), eight mountains farther on.

Near Esinceni, we visited Thomas, a man with tuberculosis. He was unable to walk. Someone asked him, "Do you love Jesus?" His face instantly lit up, and he replied, "Yes, I love Him!"

Mrs. Simelane (who went with us) walked with others forty miles over the mountains, to attend the annual

Eight mountains to reach "The Place Far Out."

(L-R) Preacher Nkambule, Mrs. Simelane,
Thomas (on mat) and Preacher Gamede

Bible week at Mhlosheni.

Malena Swalheim and Oddweig were stationed at Esinceni. Malena had been there twenty-six years. She walked all the way down the mountain to be with the school children, when they hoed the cornfield for their school fees.

When the son of the chief at Esinceni was ill, one of the chief's wives received the Lord. One day, a child came for help for her father, who seemed to be dying. The witch doctor had arrived at his kraal, but the father was a Christian, and refused to be treated by him.

It was about a five-hour walk from Esinceni to Empumakude. We used sticks to help in climbing the rocks. Oddweig was unable to walk that far on the mountains, so she stayed at Esinceni and continued on with her Bible classes.

Malena had an excellent recovery from an operation to remove cancer. Oddweig said it was like a miracle. Malena walked slowly over the mountains, but the Lord helped her get along very well. She stopped to drink from streams between the mountains. She had probably built up a resistance to their contents – just as the Africans had – from continually drinking from them.

We had left Esinceni at about 4:30 p.m., so we stayed overnight in the kraal of a fine Christian mother, whose husband had died. Her three children were Timothy, John (a herdboy) and Sesilea (who had finished one year at the Esinceni School). The widow heard footsteps around their former hut at night. So she moved and built a new hut – finishing the windbreak in one day. She was originally from Mozambique (formerly Portuguese East Africa), a little farther north. We could see it beyond a mountain range.

The doorway of our grass hut was not much higher than our knees, so we got down on our hands and knees to crawl in. There were no windows. There was a door, but when it was closed there was still quite a crack; so during the night I watched for snakes now and then, and shook the food box to scare away a mouse, which was trying to take some of its contents.

Cattle were not fed corn. It was considered to be people's food. Cows ate nice green grass. On special occasions, the people, in an unusual way, used what they had to make a floor covering – which was like nice firm linoleum when dry. It was said to keep away unwelcome insects. I once saw a woman making it. She put green cow manure into a bucket. As she stirred enough water in to make a thick mixture, her arm became green nearly up to her elbow. Then she skillfully smeared the solution over the floor. The kind widow had applied this polish to our floor. It had not become dry yet. Our hut was on a steep mountainside, so the floor was slanting. Our heads were at the higher part of our grass mat "mattress." Actually, when carrying it, as well as when sleeping on it, I found the mat was as slippery as an unbaled load of oat straw. (One time on our Illinois farm, when we brought in a load of oat straw, the hayrack came to a place where the lane sloped sideways. Soon, the straw sloped sideways, too, and slid right off the side of the rack onto the ground.) When we awoke in the morning, we discovered we had slipped down partway off the mat onto the still sticky, green floor covering – coating part of us, as well.

The widow wanted us to visit in the kraals all around there, too, but we needed to go to others that had not been reached yet.

A lady from a kraal along the way helped us carry things. She was going to one of Oddweig's Bible classes the next day. Ants were abundant in certain places in the paths across the mountaintops. At those places, people walked in grass at the side, so their bare feet would not be bitten.

Quite a few of the women were wearing some kind of ordinary cooking apron like we have. It was their custom that all the married women wear aprons. In one valley, we met an old man who was saved when Malla Moe was there.

Leaving our hut at the widow's kraal.

The day we started out from Esinceni, Oddweig saw a cobra by the water tank, and also a very poisonous green snake. We had wrapped our snakebite kit in a white towel to keep it as cool as possible, as it was supposed to be refrigerated or kept cool. Empumakude is quite high. The Swazis said no snakes were there, and indeed, we saw none at all. Monkeys came to trouble the fields at Empumakude, so people watched for them night and day, to chase them away.

We lived in the church at Empumakude. A chameleon fell from the roof just as we arrived, and then darted out through a crack when it saw us. Nice birds sang in the trees in the mornings.

Malena did not know what safety matches were. She said people were so clever in America, and so kind. They had sent her things she needed. The walls of the church were made of strong poles and mud. The roof was thatched. The ladder for thatching was made of branches, with one nail on each side, holding up each rung. There was a good-sized, flat piece of metal on the top ridge of the church, but we could still see the sky through the holes in the roof. The metal piece was not long enough to cover the holes. A small wind blew the metal piece down one evening. It was easy to replace it.

We only had a drizzle one night, so the roof did not leak too badly. We moved our mat into one corner of the church, so the rain could not drip on us.

It did not rain much, except ants (and small chunks of mud) from the cracked, well-ventilated mud walls. It was probably ants that left marks on our chests and limbs. The spots were not painful. They were only itchy. Here and there, ants ate through the papers we spread under our sleeping mat. One of us knew how to make a potassium permanganate solution. We sprinkled it over the floor. That stopped the ants.

Africans, in some areas, sprinkle potassium permanganate in their homes and fields, and plant shallots around their homes to keep snakes away. Malena had some red Jello from Norway we mixed up. The girls thought it was potassium permanganate.

We hung the bread in a sack from a crossbeam, and the ants did not find it. They found the butter easily, on the beam above the door. So we hung the butter and a jar of hamburgers out in a tree. We heated the hamburgers twice, and they kept well. It was cool in the wattle tree's shade.

There was a good-sized wattle grove around the church. I think Oddweig gave the evangelist wattle seeds, so they would have wood to build the church. There was plenty of wood. Wattle trees grow fast. They were going to redo the church walls with a substance harder than mud, from down by the river. The substance was white and looked like cement when it hardened.

There were many dry branches under the wattle trees. It

was easy to make a fire. Wattle burned quickly. It boiled water from the river almost immediately. We always drank tea. We brushed our teeth with tea water, because it was boiled. One time, a girl brushed her hair with a scrub brush.

One night, we heard a large mouse running around on the floor. When we turned on the flashlight – there was the mouse! One of the girls lifted the food box, which was sitting on two sticks, to keep it up from ants. The mouse disappeared down a hole under the box. The girl stuffed paper down the hole. The mouse never came back to run on the floor again. We were glad, because we, too, were on the floor at night.

There was a little, old, wooden table with two benches, which were rather unsteady, but so nice to have. The people kindly brought cooked porridge, and the ubiquitous sour milk, which was a good help.

One evening, a round, black pot of sour milk fell from a bench to the floor. It was only chipped a little at the top, so they could still use it all right. It was made of clay, and baked in fire. Malena asked the girls right away how badly it was broken. "It was only broken in its mouth," they replied.

One time at an evangelists' meeting, one preacher set his glasses down. The next thing they knew, a monkey had the glasses on – up in the top of a tree!

Evangelist Ntshangasi at Empumakude could only see with one eye. His glasses had a lens in only one rim. The lens looked like ordinary, flat glass. The other rim was empty. He could not see well to read.

Evangelist Ntshangasi built a kitchen with the bush knife at left (leaning against the church behind the black pot).

We were going to send him a magnifier. He had wondered if Malena knew of any old Bible available. He only had a New Testament, and it was falling apart. He used to be at Empumakude, but had been far away for a while. The chief of the area asked him to come back (as they had no evangelist), so he returned.

Lady (at right) brought us a gallon of sugar!

The evangelist brought us two goat skins. They made good rugs. His wife brought us a round, black pot of delicious, well-cooked pumpkin. Others brought us chickens, porridge, sour milk and pennies. A boy often brought milk from the kraal above us, but I just drank tea, as cows were not tested for tuberculosis. A Scandinavian missionary doctor became ill. They discovered he had tuberculosis. He had worked long hours in the tuberculosis section of a hospital with the Africans. He was so run down that he could not fight off the disease. Two-thirds of his right lung had to be removed. But he got up from bed for his wedding, and became quite well.

Ladies who brought helpful food. A small herdboy (at far right).

During the day, we went out at noon to visit in kraals. People were back in their huts from the fields by then. Three little children received the Lord in one kraal, and it was so good to see them at church on Sunday. They had to come a long ways. They looked so lost and pitiful when we first saw them, but their faces were just beaming at church. Their names were Njolonjolo, Maduna and Zilayile.

The people longed to have a school, but there was no one who could teach. On another mountain, we found a school in one

hut. There was a blackboard at one side of the room. The children had fashioned black pots of various shapes and sizes. The pots were sitting at the side in a cluster. The girl who taught there had finished

Mother (carrying baby on her back) washing at river.

sixth grade at New Haven, north of Mhlosheni. She was a fine Christian. She was concerned for her husband who was not saved. He was going to come to church Sunday morning, but some people came by going to a beer drink, and he went with them. She kept talking with him though, and was glad to have some verses we gave her from 1 Corinthians. She was not going to be able to teach the next year. The reason she could not teach anymore was because she had to do all the planting and hoeing in the fields, as well as preparing the food at home.

At a large kraal on the next mountain, the people belonged to a cult, and had signs painted on their door. No matter what the people were like, they always made us welcome to visit with them.

A grandmother and a young mother with a baby listened well at a kraal. The grandmother was very close to receiving the Lord, but she said, "I know that if I believe, I cannot return to my evil ways tomorrow." So she did not receive the Saviour then.

We were thankful some children were saved that day.

The grandmother gave us a large bowl of amahewu, a thick drink made from sour milk and corn with purple kernels. Malena drank much. I took a little – with many swallows. It was good. Malena liked it and sour milk very much. She had built up a resistance to it, as she probably had to river water. I could eat it easily, too, but wanted to avoid any harmful bacteria it might contain. Then the Swazi lady who had come with us from the church finished the amahewu – in almost no time!

On an adjacent mountain, the people were drinking beer. At the top of another mountain, we found a person who had received the Lord when the evangelist had spoken.

At another place, I told the story about a man swimming thirty feet from shore and calling out, "Which way to shore?" Two men on the shore just ignored him. "Anyone can see the shore is right over here," they said. They thought he was just trying to attract attention. But the man sank – and drowned! He seemed to be strong and swimming well, but he was swimming in the wrong direction, for he was blind! And there are people today who want to know the way to heaven, and it is our responsibility to tell them they can be saved by receiving Christ as their Saviour. Afterwards, Evangelist Ntshangasi asked where that was in the Bible. I told him it was not a story from the Bible. Maybe he thought it was in the Old Testament, which he did not have.

Another day, we found many people at a large kraal. They gathered around and stared, since they were unaccustomed to white people. They were quite decorated. The young men had long hair that was so thick, it stuck out all over. In their hair were bright beads and feathers. One had two very long, curving feathers in his hair. One man had large safety pins dangling from his earlobes. One carried a large mirror in his hand, and other accessories.

They had brought two cows to pay for a bride. They had already had the wedding, but were continuing the celebration. They butchered the two cows for a feast.

They straightened the two cowhides out in the sun to dry. They pegged the hides to the ground to stretch them – leaving a space for air between them and the ground. Women use the hides for skirts – after they rub them with coal, so they are all black. The men may wear them for clothing, too.

It was very evident it was a heathen wedding. The carryings-on were not good. They wanted us to read the Bible. So we gladly went into a hut they showed us, and as many of them as could squeezed in, too. Others sat on the ground just outside the doorway. A mat along the wall fell down behind me, but it was all right.

As we were leaving the hut to read the Bible outside so everyone could hear, a man asked where the verses were found that had been read. They were John 14:6, Acts 4:12 and Romans 1. Later, we learned that he was the bridegroom. He wanted to buy a Bible. It was so good to have a chance to talk with all those outside. These people are very straightforward in the way they talk. Romans 1 seemed to fit so well what had been going on. We hoped it spoke to them.

They were very kind to us, and just as we were going to leave, they brought us a large piece of meat! The dish it was in was so shallow that the meat draped over into the dust. So they brought a deeper dish, a pocketknife, and a tin of water to wash our hands in. The tallow hardened on the dish. The meat surely was delicious; as Wilfred Hart says – they really do know how to cook meat. The men went and sat down in the cattle kraal to eat meat, as was their custom when cattle were paid for a bride.

On the way back, we heard a strange noise over on the adjacent mountain. It was a woman running down the mountain and making that noise. It sounded like a young lion, and partly like a pig. The girls with us were very frightened. They said it was a demon-possessed person. She was thrashing from one side of a deep gully to the other, as she tumbled on down the mountain. She cried out in the bushes at the bottom, and then we saw her sitting on a stone under a tree. She came toward us and made that noise again, though not so loudly. Her eyes looked wild, with much round white surrounding the irises. She wore the paraphernalia of a witch doctor – which she was. She called to us, holding out her hands. The girls had run on down the mountain. The evangelist's wife was with us that day. She was not afraid at all, and I was not either, remembering "… greater is he that is in you, than he that is in the world" (1 John 4:4). It was a terrible sight. Malena thought it was better for us to keep going. "Stay nicely," Malena said. These are the two words Swazis speak when leaving. But the witch doctor was not able to give the customary, kind reply, "Go nicely."

It was getting dark, and we still had one more mountain to climb. That was the latest time we ever got back during that trek.

I had not learned the language well yet. When I later heard the witch doctor was calling out, "Give me! Give me!", I wished I had said, "Take Jesus, for He is the One you need!" Malena said, "It just shows the great power of Satan. You don't know what a person like that might do." Malena said there was trouble once with a demon-possessed person who would come and whistle, shout and throw ashes around. Malena said it was very, very dangerous. It shows the power of darkness. Only Christ can break it. It was good there was a Christian lady in the kraal the witch doctor came from, who could talk with her.

Earlier that day, we had been at a kraal where the people had been drinking beer. An older woman there listened intently. She said she did not have clothes to wear to church. When she heard James 2:5 – "Hearken my beloved brethren, Hath not God chosen the poor of this world rich in faith …" – and the verses before it, she marveled! She said the Bible speaks to us about the very things we need to know! We also read 1 Samuel 16:7 – "… man looketh on the outward appearance, but the Lord looketh on the heart"; as well as "… We ought to obey God rather than men" (Acts 5:29). She said she was still going to think some more before she believed. Malena said it was not too surprising that these, who had never heard the gospel before, wanted to think more.

After a day of trekking, if we were not too tired and it was not drizzling, we went to the stream at the foot of our mountain to bathe and wash clothes. The water was so refreshing. Many trees made it cool. The water seemed to be coming from a spring back under large boulders.

One night, Malena forgot to wind her watch, so we guessed the time. We could tell the days all right, remembering every other day we took paludrine to prevent malaria. Oddweig thought her malaria had recurred some. I took paludrine two weeks, and then took three camoquin pills the next day. There were mosquitoes where we washed, but we thanked the Lord they did not bite us. Spectacular "fever trees," with brilliant, yellowish-green bark and leaves, grew in some malaria areas.

We often heard herdboys playing by cracking and cracking leather thongs they attached to sticks.

Africans shout from mountain to mountain to converse. It is amazing how loudly the Lord enables them to shout. It is a great blessing. It saves much time. They do not have to trek all the way down their mountain, through the brush or river at its foot, and climb far up on their neighbors' mountain to communicate.

Malena used to go with Malla Moe in her gospel wagon drawn by sixteen donkeys. One donkey was named "James" and another "Pony." There was a picture of Malla Moe and Malena with the King of Swaziland's mother in the Sunday School Times in America. Malena kept telling us interesting things. She said during a war with Russia a young, Christian Finnish soldier died. Two hundred people saw an angel come straight down from heaven and take him, though his body still remained. It happened very quickly. They were so shocked. It was a great sermon to them.

Malla kept telling Malena she should go home and tell the people in Norway about the Lord, because there were no Christians in Malena's family. When Malena went on furlough, a good number of Norwegians became Christians.

In 1941, when Oddweig was on furlough in Norway, Malena was alone at Esinceni.

Helen (a girl converted at Esinceni) took teacher training at Bremersdorp. She taught at our Mhlosheni School. She became sick with malaria at Empumakude. During this time, Malena was awakened one night when she heard something like angels singing. She could not see them, but it seemed like there was just a waving up and down above the doorway. They sang a hymn in Zulu and in English. Malena said she was not afraid at all. It just seemed very wonderful – so peaceful and beautiful. She listened and learned the words.

They came and sang several nights. Malena would lie and listen to them. She said she wondered if some missionary was dying. She thought of Mary Danielson in Southern Rhodesia. Mary's husband, Rudy, had had malaria and died there. Mary's baby was to be born about that time, and Malena started praying for Mary.

The last night Malena heard the angels sing, they stopped suddenly – and never came back again. Someone came and told Malena that Helen had died. Malena realized it was just at the time the angels had stopped singing.

One year, because the Empumakude evangelist had died, Elsa Swalheim (Malena's sister) and I went out from Esinceni to Empumakude. To make less to carry, we took plastic spoons and round tins for plates. Elsa took a tiny comb for her long hair. I wore gym shoes to avoid carrying galoshes, not realizing fungus will grow when air-tight, plastic toes of shoes remain damp for some time after a rain. In later years, one big toenail had to be removed surgically, but the Lord wonderfully healed it.

On the way, we came to a small kraal where they were cooking food,

One of Elsa's round tins used for a plate.

which appeared to be green weeds. A child was leading a blind man at one place.

We reached Empumakude and stayed in the church. There were a few backless benches. Each end of a bench had a short, rectangular board fastened vertically under it to hold the bench up nicely – usually. One bench was a sideways teeter-totter (because one attached board slanted to the right, and the other, to the left). But that bench stayed still when we placed a normal bench beside it. This made a nice bed to move onto, when ants ate through one of our grass mats on the floor and bit sharply.

Elsa and visitors. Evangelist's wife (at far right).

On one visit, we met a lady who asked, "Do you have clothes (to give away)?" She was wearing nice, strong clothing. "Do you have Jesus?" we asked. "Yes!" she said. When she heard He is better than extra clothes – clothes can be lost, she agreed, saying, "Yes!" Things of the world perish. Jesus is eternal. "Jesus Christ the same yesterday, today, and for ever" (Hebrews 13:8).

At one kraal we read, "Two women shall be grinding at the mill; the one shall be taken, and the other left … Therefore be ye also ready: for in such an hour as ye think not the Son of man cometh" (Matthew 24:41, 44). We said, "We do not know when Jesus is coming. He may come today! Wouldn't you like to receive Jesus as your Saviour, so that you can go to heaven, too?" A mother, with a long hairpin in her hair sat, listening intently. The other mother sat by the hut, uninterested. Except for the humming of insects, all was quiet. We sat in silence in front of our hostesses, on the grass mats they had kindly spread out for us when we came. It was good – here we had found one who was thinking of what the Lord has done for us. (There were many people at another kraal where we had just been, but their thoughts were on the things of this life.)

The stillness was broken, as the mother who was listening intently opened her lips, and expressed her desire to be amongst those who love the Lord and His appearing.

Mother with long hairpin.

A young girl approached from behind the garden fence by the papaw (papaya) tree.

"Do you know the way to heaven?" I asked her.

"No," she answered, stirring one of her round, black pots of beer.

But before the sun disappeared that day, she also was numbered amongst those of whom the Lord said, "And they shall be mine ... in that day when I make up my jewels ..." (Malachi 3:17). We thanked the Lord He had helped more to receive Him before sunset.

On our way back to Esinceni, it began to rain. The people had given us a hen. She was resting comfortably in a strong-handled, narrow,

Girl by the papaw tree who received Christ.

neatly-woven grass bag I was carrying. The path was rough and the rocks became slippery. As we went down one long, steep rock, my gym shoes suddenly slid. The hen remained intact in her slim, warm nest, as the basket flew up into the air, making a complete circle – in the awesome spectacle of the rapid human descent, and high-speed hen ascent!

We continued our journey. When we reached the kind widow's kraal, where we had stayed the first night, we met Christians coming from Esinceni. It was so good to see them. It made one's heart rejoice, and eyes brim with tears, to see the miracle of the happy faces and transformed lives of saved people. Four of them had been baptized that day.

Steep, slippery rocks are behind bushes (at right).

We noticed a strong odor coming from a neighboring hut. We went and found a lady who had a badly infected hand. It was very swollen and discolored with gangrene. She had been so frightened that she ran away from the doctor at Bremersdorp. She had regularly attended Oddweig's Bible classes. She said she felt she must hold tightly to the Lord. Oddweig told her the Lord could hold her more tightly and with greater power than her own. Isaiah 41:10 says, "Fear thou not; for I am with thee: be not dismayed; for I am thy God: I will strengthen thee; yea, I will help thee; yea, I will uphold thee with the right hand of my righteousness." We were comforted to know that now that Oddweig was back from furlough, she would probably get it treated.

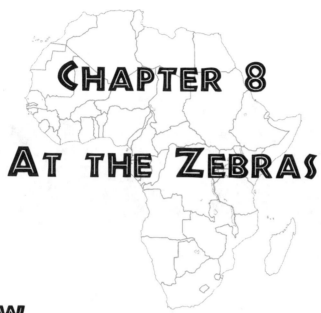

CHAPTER 8

AT THE ZEBRAS

We looked forward eagerly to the closing of school, for then we could visit the people "At the Zebras" (Madubeni), where there was much darkness.

The Lord provided a place to stay. Letters had come from two Christians there:

Yes, Nkosazana, we received the one (letter) *that came from you. We were very happy. I have sent the letter to Madubeni. They say they will receive you. They say they can be happy when that time comes in December. They say they will come out and wait for you at the station. We thank very much for the stamps and envelopes. The church at Madubeni greets with hymn 107 in the hymnbook. And I am greeting with hymn 3* ("Now He dwells in my heart – my Friend"). *I am thankful for the privilege of having fellowship with our Friend. Now they will wait for the day of the 15th December* (Summer time in the southern hemisphere). *Stay nicely, our Nkosazana.*

It is I,

Mrs. S. Simelane

Bush country with distant mountains.

They would walk about seven miles through the bush to come out and wait for us at the bus stop.

Then came the second letter:

Yes, Nkosazana, I read your letter which said you will come. Really we can be happy if you can come, our Nkosazana. If the Lord is willing you can come, in His strength only. Really we are longing for that day. I am greeting you with hymn 67 in the hymnbook, and we want you to stay until January 4.

"This River" and her baby at the bus stop with Ida.

So in December, Georgena Cole (from Canada), Ida, the Swazi orphan (now nine years old), and I set out for northern Swaziland, to stay at the Nhlengethwas' kraal and visit in other kraals.

"There are cattle everywhere – but not the gospel!" said

Nhlengethwas and visitors at their kraal.

Mr. Nhlengethwa with oxen.

Mrs. Nhlengethwa holding the oxen's "reins."

"Grope–In–The–Dark" leading the oxen.

Samuel leading the oxen.

Samuel took off the oxen's yoke.

Calves behind the resting plow.

Mr. Nhlengethwa. It was noticeable there were many cattle. The Nhlengethwas had over seventy, themselves.

Plowing was only done until about 8 a.m., and then it was stopped for the day, so the oxen would not get overheated.

One of the main (earthly) occupations was to be an inspector at a dip, where cattle were taken down through a disinfectant in water to rid them of harmful insects.

Pretending to put "cattle" (nuts) in the dip they dug in the ground.

The Nhlengethwas' cattle knew their names. When herding the cattle, herdboys spoke to them by name – calling out to turn them back if they were going the wrong way.

Cows came up to be tied by their horns to a tree when they

Eight oxen yoked together.

Cow tied to tree for milking.

We all took turns milking.

*"Cares For"
getting a cow
up to milk.*

were milked. When a boy finished milking one cow, he called the name of the one he wanted next, and she came walking up!

In Isaiah 1:3–4 the Lord had to say, "The ox knoweth his owner ... but ... Israel doth not know, my people doth not consider ... they have forsaken the Lord ...". We must know the Lord to go to heaven. John 17:3 says, "And this is life eternal, that they might know thee the only true God, and Jesus Christ, whom thou hast sent."

While visiting in kraals, we met one boy who did not know what the Bible was. We were thankful to be there, so we could tell him.

Another time, we came to a boy and a girl, Ruth, with such longing in her eyes, who was happy to converse.

*The calf was
brought to
milk first;
otherwise,
the cow
would not
give any milk.*

"Is the little boy your brother?" I asked.

"My sister's brother," she replied. Her father probably had more than one wife.

"Where is she today?"

"At the cows."

"Can you read?"

"No, I am one who herds cattle."

"Can anyone at home read?"

"Job."

"Does he go to Sunday School?"

"He doesn't go."

"You could invite him to come next week!"

"He says never will he go to Sunday School." Hearing this made us sad.

At one kraal, a number of men were sitting in a circle with a beer pot. Their long hair was sticking out, as they had filled

Swazis only strip the cow. When I showed her our way of milking, Saraphina just smiled and kept on deftly stripping.

it with soapsuds for decoration. We began to explain the way to heaven. Their wives began to gather to listen to the word of God, too. One man was the brother of Chief Khisimus. He had a regal bearing. His son's name was "Cares For." "We are just beginning to understand," they said. "If you would come

"Cares For" freeing a cow. Ida threw a thong up around a branch to make a swing.

and tell us again, we would understand better." One of the men loosened a little watch hanging on the skins he was wearing. He asked, "What is the right time?" as he tried to loosen the watch. It was a good opportunity to also say that the right time for them was – really – the time to receive salvation now from the Lord. They understood, though they did not respond to the gospel that day.

Different Swazis went with us each day. Samson, the Nhlengethwas' oldest son, lived at the next kraal. The first day, Samson's wife went with us. We stopped at a kraal where some mothers and their children gathered to listen. After we finished reading the Bible, Samson's wife took a stiff grass stem and held it up like a candle, saying, "Now the light has come. Now you have heard. You must receive the Lord. If you don't, then in the end, the Lord will ask you, 'What about the day when the daughters of the King came and told you the way to heaven?' "

Back at the Nhlengethwas' kraal, three children received the Lord. It was too far for them to walk to the church service held under a tree. The brother of Frances, a student at our Mhlosheni

School, had built a store there in the bush for the people. He had started a Sunday School under this tree by his store. Their father had tuberculosis and had just come home from the hospital. What an encouragement it was to meet with the Christians for their service. It was an hour's walk to where they met.

Samson Nhlengethwa spoke at the church service, saying, "Before we knew about it, God had this tree and its shade arranged as a hospital for souls!" Then he read from John 3,

Samson, Try, Mrs. Nhlengethwa, "Grope–In– The–Dark" and Martha

starting with verse 16, and said, "It is foolish for a blind person to refuse a guide." (A Swazi blind person is led by a stick. A child leads the blind person, who holds onto the other end of the stick.) Samson continued, "If a blind person refuses a guide, he may go off the road, enter into a gully and fall down into it! Jesus is the One Who is holding the stick for us. It is wise to follow His leading. If they want milk at a kraal, I take them my cow. They milk her, but she is mine. Whenever I want to, I can come and take her. Jesus can take souls whenever He likes. Don't mind the mistakes. I did not get a chance to learn, but I love to speak for the Lord."

A row of heathen people passed by (on a path in the long grass) going to a beer drink. They did not want to come to listen to the good words of eternal life. Before the believers departed after the service, one of them asked, "Who will we remember above all?" "Jesus!" came the quick response.

They wanted to build a church, so they could meet when it rained, too. But Chief Khisimus was a drunkard, and had not yet granted permission. They wanted to build a school, too. The Nhlengethwas' younger son, Samuel, walked to the Esinceni School, eleven miles away. He was in second grade.

Samuel letting a calf out.

When we reached home, Ida said the children had had Sunday School. "Cares For," the nephew of Chief Khisimus, was there. They prayed, learned a memory verse, and sang, "He set me free. I was blind, but now I see. I will never forget the day when He took my sins away. Jesus set me free." They also sang, "Open your heart; there is Someone knocking. Open your heart that He may enter."

Saraphina, the oldest daughter at home at Nhlengethwas, went visiting with us. One afternoon, on the way home she was so happy – saying, "Now they have <u>heard</u> – even though some have not received the Lord yet."

One of the huts at Nhlengethwas was deteriorating, so posts were set in for a new hut. A string stretched across from the corner posts showed how deep to dig the holes, so all the poles would be even at their tops for the roof.

Saraphina by posts to replace the deteriorating hut.

The Nhlengethwas setting in a post. More are at right on the sled.

A grandmother came to a kraal where we were visiting. She was carrying on her back "This Winter," a girl about eleven

"This Winter." The New Year's feast's calf's skull was fastened to the tree using the ladder (L). They gave us the calf skin.

years old. The girl was thin. They said she had become sick, and was just getting weaker and weaker. They thought she was going to die. But she was very cheerful, for she was a Christian. Ida was praying for her that night, that she might get well – "Or," she prayed, "if she is taken to be with Thee, it is all right. It isn't a burden – only joy – because there are no burdens with Thee!" The Lord healed "This Winter."

"No, I haven't received the Lord, but my parents gave me to Him when I was little," said Luke, the oldest child at Nhlengethwas' kraal. "You must receive Him for yourself," we explained, giving him a tract. The next night, when we were gathered together to worship the Lord, Luke stood up and said, "I love the Lord!" (a way they say they have received Christ as their Saviour). Later, we found him reading *Pilgrim's Progress* in Zulu, which he had purchased from a Bible student, who came to the kraal for the New Year's Day service. A wooden spoon for a feast may be as large as a saucer, with a yard-long handle.

Large feast spoon. Visitor (at right) has mud in her hair.

Many came to listen as Enoch, a Bible student, preached at the New Year's feast. Enoch and two other Bible students were building a church six miles away.

Lady (at left) gave up snuff and had a Sunday School at her kraal.

The people built a strong, flat wooden "sled" to haul water drums or thatching grass. Holes were carved out along the edges of the sled. Ends of poles were set into the holes to make erect

Loading thatching grass onto sled.

"sideboards." There were no nails. So thongs were used or grass was braided into sturdy rope, to attach to supporting poles to keep thatching grass from sliding off, as the strong oxen sped along on the sometimes slanting, sandy road. Braided grass held each bundle of thatching grass together.

Oxen pulled the thatching grass to the new church site.

The little boys played with a miniature "ox sled." Cornstalks, arranged like a corduroy road, formed its floor. It was pulled by a braided grass "rope." It was triangular in shape. The wide part at the back of the sled was about fifteen inches across. They pulled things around in their sled.

It was not easy to obtain water. In some places, the people had to travel for miles to reach a river. Oddweig had one cup of water for brushing her teeth and bathing, at one kraal.

One day, seeing six oxen being yoked to the sled to get two drums of water, Ida asked, "May I go with the sled?" But she quickly added, "I do want to go to take the gospel, though!" – in case it might only be possible to go on one of the trips. The people said it would be unsafe to go with the oxen, so we set out happily with our Bibles, to the kraals. "Why couldn't I go with the oxen?" asked Ida. I explained it was too dangerous. The oxen went fast. Sleds tipped, so it was easy to fall off. Jesus said, "… If any man will come after me, let him deny himself …" (Matthew 16:24). "For my thoughts are not your thoughts, neither are your ways my ways, saith the Lord. For as the heavens are higher than the earth, so are my ways higher than your ways, and my thoughts than your thoughts" (Isaiah 55:8–9). Before long, we saw how the Lord had marvelously protected Ida. We came to a kraal where a woman's foot was painfully swollen. She was injured riding on a water sled. A long, deep cut on the side of her foot was not healing well. Ida could see how the

Lord rewarded her by keeping her from being hurt – when she chose to serve Him, rather than to please herself.

Phungandlu was herding cattle. He listened to some verses, set down his spear, and asked the Lord to save him.

The Lord helped Phonono to receive Him, too. Her baby girl's name was "Small One." It was a blessing Phonono could go back in peace to her home called "The Place of Wrath."

A group of Christian children listened to the first chapters of Daniel, as we sat under a mountainside tree. A

Phonono and her baby.

heathen man came along with his hand mirror hanging at his side. Perhaps he used the mirror to position the feather in his hair. Woven wires on each side of the mirror kept it from breaking. We read verses explaining how to be saved. After a time, the man rose to leave.

"It's far to where I am going!" he announced, and prepared to be on his way. We said, "It may not be far – if you should die right away. We never know how long we may live. We may die very suddenly! Jesus said, '... be ye also ready ...' (Matthew 24:44)." The man realized he was not ready to go into eternity. He became ready – praying and asking the Lord to forgive his sins and be his Saviour.

Green mealies are tender, young ears of corn. Swazis enjoy cooking and eating them very much. Mrs. Nhlengethwa said, "The Bible is like green mealies – fresh always!" One morning, she took us to the pond to show us the place for washing. She walked ahead with a tree branch, swishing the heavy dew off the tall grass on either side of the path. I had a navy blue, seersucker dress, as there was no way to iron clothes. The dress had a pretty, white stripe down the front, and white stripes around the sleeves and pockets. The water in the small pond where we

Martha and Ida by the dress with white stripes.

could wash clothes was thick and brown. At first, it was hard to immerse the bright, cheerful white trim – never to be white again! But it was just an earthly thing – not important at all, compared to precious souls being reached! Luke 12:48 tells us that "… unto whomsoever much is given, of him shall much be required …". Salvation is much. A bright, white trim would go to dust, anyway. It was nothing compared to having eternal life in heaven, and telling others how to obtain it.

One day, it rained. They immediately set up a six-foot eaves trough from a rectangular roof to a barrel – to collect every possible drop. Water ran down in trenches from the huts to a depression they had dug in the center of the kraal – to make another good water supply.

Georgena, whose brother and family were missionaries in South America, read from the Bible to an illiterate person who came to the Nhlengethwas. She was reading at the dry depression in the center of the kraal one sunny day.

Georgena reading to visitor.

The children roasted grasshoppers and sparrows to eat. They also cracked nuts and picked out the nutmeats with four-inch-long thorns.

Birds in dish a herdboy got with his slingshot.

Roasting sparrows by the cattle kraal where we read the Bible daily.

This girl picked out nutmeats with a thorn.

Sorting nuts.

Ida removed a thorn from "Grope–In– The–Dark's" foot.

One day, there was a train of children going along – Phumaphi, Siphiwe and Ida. Each had a blanket. Ida was almost hopping up and down on tiptoe with joy. They were going to the mango tree. Soon, Martha (Nhlengethwas' daughter) and Ida were enjoying mangoes by our hut with Georgena.

Enjoying mangoes. Georgena is holding a tin for drinking.

We had a box of powdered milk my sister had provided. We also put Kool-Aid in boiled water and added sugar for energy. Later, when Georgena got back to her simple, concrete rondoval home at her mission station in southern Swaziland, she exclaimed, "This is a palace!"

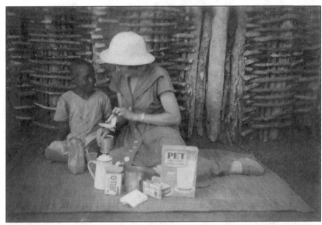

The box of powdered milk.

As we were coming back from a visit at the chief's kraal, Mrs. Nhlengethwa pointed to a long mark in the soil, which went diagonally across the path in front of us. She said it was made by a mamba going down to drink water in a pond. "It was made by a young one. But they are poisonous, too," she said. We thanked God it had already gone past, and had not come upon us suddenly.

One day, Georgena sat by our hut with Martha, Ida,

"Grope–In– The–Dark" (by Barkie, the dog) enjoying a feast rib.

"Try" and "Grope–In–The–Dark." "Try's" parents worked in Johannesburg, so there was no one to care for him at home.

When we were around the fire one night, "Grope–In–The–Dark" asked, "Where do the angels live?" "Try" was counting the stars and got to "10" – as far as he could count.

They have beautiful smiles, but the custom was to look solemn for a photo. (L-R) Try, Mrs. Nhlengethwa, "Grope–In–The–Dark" and Martha.

One day, someone under the cattle kraal tree was singing into a hollowed-out gourd, "Count your many blessings." It was young Ida. She often prayed for the chief's blind headman (we had met the first day), who had not become a Christian yet: "That he might see that which is invisible!"

Oddweig said to Malla Moe, "I can't sing." Malla said, "You don't need to – the Africans can!" Indeed, they can – and do – marvelously! The Lord enables them to sing with beautiful harmony and tremendous volume. They can sing a hymn they have never heard before, after hearing it sung only once! There is no piano. Someone begins a hymn in a service. If it is not known who will start the hymn, sometimes two will start it at the same time – each on perfect pitch!

If people have shoes, they often carry them when going to church, and then put them on when they get there. Walking long distances over grass and stones wears shoes out.

One week, we started early in the morning to attend the service at Esinceni, about twelve miles away. We climbed a mountain at the end of the journey to reach the church. We had

Ida, by thick tree leaves where women fatten soft, several-inch-long caterpillars to eat.

become very thirsty in the noonday heat. Spouts led from the eaves of the mission home into the top of a large, round water tank. We opened the tank's tap. The water was cool, as it was under shady trees. We kept filling our cupped hands with the refreshing water, and drinking it – for a long, long time. Weeks later, back at Mhlosheni, there was a knock at the door. An African, passing through, asked for a drink of water. I hastened to get an abundant supply – remembering a long journey causes great thirst. He may have walked for many miles. He began to drink. After some time, at last he said, "Ngikholiwe!" Ngikholiwe means "I am satisfied!" It also means "I have believed!" It is the very word Swazis use when they have received Christ as their Saviour! They stand up in church and announce, "Ngikholiwe!" ("I am satisfied!") It is the greatest thing that satisfies us in this life – to know we have been delivered from hell forever, so we can eternally be in heaven, because we have taken of the water of life freely (Revelation 22:17). Jesus said, "... If any man thirst, let him come unto me, and drink" (John 7:37). "... the

Lord shall satisfy thy soul ..." (Isaiah 58:11).

One day, we met a young man, Samson. He carried a mirror, as young men often did. His hair was thoroughly decorated with beads. He listened to the way of salvation attentively. "We are in darkness," he said, "and Christians say to come to the path of light. I do want to have eternal life. I do want to receive Jesus as my Saviour. I can come to your kraal tomorrow afternoon!" We mentioned the uncertainty of life, and that Jesus said, "... be ye also ready: for in such an hour as ye think not the Son of man cometh" (Matthew 24:44). So he did not wait, but received the Lord that day.

"I am not a Christian, but I want to be one," someone said. Others who put their trust in the Lord were Janetta, "Fetters" and "Stay-in-Jail." Mr. Nhlengethwa was so happy about "Stay-in-Jail's" conversion. He was Nhlengethwas' nearest neighbor.

A boy named "Chief" was pulling his "wagon," made of a forked branch on wheels that were carved out of wood. "Chief" wanted to receive the Lord.

"I don't know how to pray," he said. We read helpful Bible verses. "Chief" prayed, asking the Lord to save him.

"Where are you going now?" I asked.

"Home," he replied.

"I mean, at the end of your life on earth?"

"To heaven!" he said, smiling.

We thanked God for those who put their trust in Him. So often, we thought with thanksgiving of those who had been praying for the area, as we saw ready responses to the gospel.

"I am the only one remaining in my family who is not a Christian," said Mfanzane, who came over to the road where we were waiting for the bus on our last day at Madubeni. "My mother is saved. My wife is saved. I, only, remain. But how can I be saved? I don't have clothes!" he said earnestly, indicating his bare chest – "And I am a poor person." We read from 1 Samuel 16:7 – "... the Lord seeth not as man seeth; for man looketh on the outward appearance, but the Lord looketh on the heart." We also read, "Hearken, my beloved brethren, Hath not

God chosen the poor of this world rich in faith …?" (James 2:5). Mfanzane understood and came to the Lord, and happily left for home.

After a time, his father came hurrying toward us through the bush, and began talking excitedly. He said Mfanzane had come and told him what he had done.

"I told him I would give him my vest," the father exclaimed, "if he would come to church! It has been good you have come. When the bus comes, let's be singing a hymn, so they will know we are Christians."

We were singing a hymn when the bus came.

"Blessed be the Lord God … who only doeth wondrous things. And blessed be his glorious name for ever: and let the whole earth be filled with his glory …" (Psalm 72:18–19).

CHAPTER 9

THE PLACE OF THE WILDCAT

On one trek, we went to "The Place of the Wildcat." Annie and another schoolgirl from Mhlosheni were happy to go along. When we boarded the African bus with a pile of tracts and handed the driver one, he said, "Here comes the Bible again! This paper explains the way to heaven. Be sure everyone gets one!" The passengers had other things, too: a big bush knife, a small door, a hoe, a hen in a box, and a sickle resting around someone's neck.

The Place of the Wildcat was a benighted area, where the gospel was much needed. We had reached kraals four miles from there before, and had seen three people who had come out from the Place of the Wildcat. Some had put cornstalks in holes pierced in their earlobes.

We stayed at a grandmother's kraal. She invited neighbors to come each evening to worship the Lord. "Where did this

Wooden plugs are fitted into ear lobes.

white one come from?" someone inquired. The grandmother said, "These are the girls of prayer. They came on the bus and then took the feet from Sipofaneni. The Lord knows. There is nothing too hard for Him!"

On the first day's trek, a cobra appeared by the path. But it stayed in the bush. After that, we made sure we took the snakebite kit along each time.

Three older girls listened to the gospel at one kraal, but when asked if they would like to receive the Lord, they were just quiet. One of the girls from Mhlosheni was telling some children the Wordless Book Story. The three girls went and listened to her.

"Murderer," a strange name for a bright boy of about seven, said, "I don't have any father, and I don't have any mother." We explained the

The grandmother at the kraal.

gospel to him. He received Christ. So now he has the greatest Father of all! Timothy, an older boy from "The Place of Love," who became a Christian a few moments later, said he would take "Murderer" to church.

Suddenly, the three older girls came hurrying back over, saying they wanted to receive Christ now! There was much thanksgiving to God.

One night, our guide for the day came to the Lord. Her husband was a Christian, and she knew how to read. No one else knew how to read – not even the leader in the church, who said, "I just say what is in my head." So it was a blessing our guide had come to the area, for she could read the Bible for them all.

One night, a mother was nearly bitten by a cobra. She felt the cold snake against her foot. She was not a Christian. She was so thankful her life was spared, so she could still receive the Saviour – and she did!

A fire (made on the ground) cooked ground corn porridge in a large, black pot. In the darkness, Annie lit a strong grass stem in the fire. To see whether the water was boiling, or the porridge was cooked – and not running over, she held the burning grass under the lid she had lifted.

Cooking over a fire in daytime.

When we emerged from our hut in the morning, they asked, "Have you gotten up?" This was a customary morning greeting.

When entering a kraal to visit, we approached a hut, stood at the side of the doorway, and said, "Ngqo! Ngqo!" It sounds like "No" with a loud click for the "q." To knock on grass would not be heard! If the people were outdoors when we arrived and saw us they paid no attention, at first. They wanted us to feel

Annie read the Bible on a good tree-branch seat.

we were part of the family – not strangers! After awhile, they greeted, saying, "We're seeing each other!"

As we reached one kraal, a Swazi going visiting with us said, "Come and choose the Living One!" The people put clothes on the children when the Bible was going to be read. When we left kraals, the people kindly said, "Go nicely!" We responded, "Stay nicely!"

We met a child named "Trouble." He said he was not a Christian, but we hoped he would become one of those strong Christians, of whom the Lord said, "… To him that overcometh will I give … a new name …" (Revelation 2:17).

The names of some children we met were "Squealy," "Unhappy," "It's Cold" and "Make Progress." A boy came running down the road, rolling the rim of a wheel with a stick. He said he did not have any name. He seemed never to have heard the gospel.

Squealy (in the center)

He said he did want eternal life in heaven, but was not ready to receive it that day.

On the road, we met an elderly man carrying home on his shoulders two large branches, for fuel to make fires. "The white child speaks!" he exclaimed, when he heard 1 Corinthians 3:16–17 and Philippians 4:13. He soon understood it is <u>God's word</u> that speaks. He said he had put his trust in the Lord, but had taken to drinking beer. This happens where people cannot read and have no one to read the Bible to them. A man nearby had tobacco rolled in a piece of paper above his ear. When he heard the verses, he threw the tobacco away. These were the verses they heard: "Know ye not that ye are the temple of God and that the Spirit of God dwelleth in you? If any man defile the temple of God, him shall God destroy; for the temple of God is holy, which temple ye are" and "I can do all things through Christ which strengtheneth me."

Women carrying branches for fuel.

A radiant Christian in a nearby store was rejoicing the gospel had reached Africa. He said, "Before the gospel came, we used to kill each other like animals! I was going to be a witch doctor." Then he explained how God saved him. He, too, had not had much Bible teaching, however. When asked where he attended church, he brought out a shiny pin, which seemed very precious to him. He did not know the meaning of the strange etching on it. We did not know what it meant either. We read Philippians 3:18–19: "(For many walk, of whom I have told you often, and now tell you even weeping, <u>that they are the enemies of the cross of Christ … who mind earthly things.</u>)" He was very thankful to hear these verses, and realized we must cling to Christ – not things.

The kraal where we had actually planned to stay was some miles farther into the bush. But the mother there had to take a very sick child to the doctor. We were glad two young people from her family came to visit us in the kraal where we did stay. We read Haggai 1:2–10, and were thankful the Lord helped them see the importance of making a new church building. White ants had demolished the old one.

The Lord helped explain the way to heaven to a young man carrying a knobkerrie weapon. His hair was parted in the center. Soapsuds fluffed his hair out at the sides. He said, "I understand it all. Maybe He will save me. I must think about it, though. It is so important. The thing is, I am not married yet. If I had a wife, she could pray for me, and I could become a Christian." We read Romans 14:12 – "So then every one of us shall give account of himself to God."

We had a happy visit in the kraal of a Christian chief. He was quite old and weak, but very happy in the Lord. The grandmother who took us to various kraals was his sister.

A number of people had gathered at the last kraal where we visited. Their unsaved grandfather had just died. We read John 14:1–6 and Matthew 24:3, 36–42 and 44, and Hypersia, a girl about eighteen, said she wanted to receive Christ. "Will you pray for me?" she asked. We considered Romans 14:12, and that if a child is very thirsty he is not helped if someone else drinks water for him. I remembered the day Miss Edith Torrey explained Acts 16:30–31 to us at school, and mentioned that I did not ask a friend to pray for me, but immediately prayed to God myself, asking Him to save my soul. Hypersia understood, and did so, too.

We read to her Romans 10:9–10 – "That if thou shalt confess with thy mouth the Lord Jesus, and shalt believe in thine heart that God hath raised him from the dead, thou shalt be saved. For with the heart man believeth unto righteousness: and with the mouth confession is made unto salvation." Miss Torrey had told us the keeper of the prison brought Paul and Silas out "… and said, Sirs, what must I do to be saved? And they said, believe on the Lord Jesus Christ, and thou shalt be saved, and thy house" (Acts 16:30–31). When I returned a little later, Hypersia was already reading verses to Dinah, another young girl, and Dinah, too, received the Lord! When talking with people waiting at the bus stop, we heard them ask the grandmother (at whose kraal we had stayed) about us. "What are they doing here?" they asked. "They are people like us," she replied, and she began to explain about us. We rejoiced they could see the love of the Lord.

Zulu women have large headdresses.

We had such happy times of fellowship when the children, grandchildren and neighbors joined us in worshiping Him in the evenings.

Zulu women wore large headdresses. They sometimes stuffed the headdress frameworks with burlap and red clay,

"Big Grass" with her baby "Pretty Country" on her back.

(L-R) "Set Alight,"
"Cares For," "The
World Goes Round"
and Macoco

Long hairpins help to
scratch the scalp.

"She Succeeds"
behind her mother,
who wears metal
ankle bands.

if there was not enough hair to fill them. At night, they slept with wooden "pillows" under their necks to keep the shape of the headdresses.

One Zulu woman in a hospital bed had her neck "resting" (?) on the foot-high metal framework at the head of her bed.

Near the Tugela River, "Set Alight," Macoco and two children wanted gospel tracts. They used long hairpins to scratch their scalps when they became itchy.

"She Succeeds" and her mother listened to the gospel. Her mother had metal bands above her ankles.

CHAPTER 10

THE PLACE OF DAWNING

The Lord guided so that a permit was granted to live in Zululand in 1965. This was a great blessing, for in those days, a permit was refused to even allow a missionary to enter the reserve area to <u>visit</u>!

Only the New Testament had been printed in the Zulu new orthography, so the Lord helped us compile a concordance for it first. This took seven years of our time in Swaziland. During those seven years, the Old Testament was printed in the Zulu new orthography. The Old Testament is three times longer. Our Field Council did not want it to take twenty-one more years to complete the Old Testament concordance, so with the Lord's guidance, I left teaching and went to our Ekuseni Mission School in Zululand, to work on it there. Some of the 300 children in the school were eager to help, so it only took fifteen more years to complete the concordance for the entire Bible.

Roma Belsher, from Portland, Oregon, lived with me at Ekuseni, "The Place of Dawning." The people named it this because when the gospel came, it was like Isaiah 9:2 says, "The people that walked in darkness have seen a great light, they that dwell in the land of the shadow of death, upon them hath the light shined."

Roma operated a clinic for the Zulus. The district surgeon came each Thursday. One day, he brought us a huge bunch of bananas. The people had given him several whole stalks, and he could not use them all!

One day, Zulus in a kraal east of us sent lots of sweet potatoes and a big cabbage. When families butchered, they sent us some meat, too. We were so thankful. One day, the Mousebird family sent us meat. So the Mousebirds were the "ravens" who brought it that time. One time, it rained many days. Cattle had no barns for shelter. We found a cow, belonging to the teacher's family, lying flat on the road – unable to breathe much longer. We quickly told the family. They were thankful to know, as they had not noticed it. They butchered the cow immediately, and gratefully sent us some of the meat.

We were marooned for some time at Ekuseni, as a large pond had formed across the road some distance away. The bus could not get in to bring mail or supplies to Ekuseni. We were glad when the Zulus told us they ate our bread, saying, "We knew you wouldn't mind." Isaac Bridegroom was the preacher at Ekuseni. The church services began at 12:30 p.m. and closed about 3:30 p.m. Sunday School was earlier.

Friday afternoons, I had Scripture class for the third, fourth and fifth grade children. The Lord helped a good number of the children to receive Him. It was such a joy to study the Bible with them. One day, sixty-five children came. The blackboard erasers were like beanbags – cloth filled with material and stitched shut. As I was standing near the front row of children one day, a girl bent down and lightly touched my white sock at the tip of my sandal, to see what it was like. I stood very still, so

Friday Scripture class at right of cactus plant.

as not to frighten her.

Many knew the answers well to Genesis questions. We had Hebrews 10:4 for a memory verse: "For it is not possible that the blood of bulls and of goats should take away sins." I asked why we do not build altars and make sacrifices now, as Noah, Abraham and others did. Right away, Eunice Laughter responded, "Because Jesus has died for us!" And Eunice was so young; I did not know this until I was seventeen.

On rainy days, the children came in early to Scripture class, so we played guessing names by filling in letters on blank blackboard spaces (N O A H). They enjoyed this so much. The one who guessed the last blank chose the next name to guess. One little boy chose "Abednego."

"Trust," a third grade boy said, "I don't know whether Jesus loves me." He soon found out from Bible verses, and received Christ as his Saviour.

One child said he did not know the way to heaven. His name was "One–Who–Defends–The–Sinner." We read Romans 3:23–24 – "For all have sinned, and come short of the glory of God; Being justified freely by his grace through the redemption that is in Christ Jesus." "We haven't sinned, and now it says we've sinned!" the boy exclaimed. "Who can forgive us in the world?" he queried, and then answered his own question, "It is Jesus!"

Tobias Jail brought us a pan of papaws. He was the most faithful one in the Friday Bible class.

Some of the names of the children in the class were: Abednego, Blessing, English, Faithful, Mispah, Lazarus, Eliphaz, Redeemed, Mirriam Thorntree, Tobias Leopard, Tryphena Mousebird, Zephaniah Cuttlefish, Caused–To–Be–Happy, Consider–Him Buffalo and Rebekah At–The–Gate.

One day, Agnes came – very concerned about her unsaved father, the chief of a large area. We gave her "The Way of Salvation," which she mailed to him.

Another girl, "One–Who–Is–Faithful" said, "Nkosazana, I am asking where the hymn is that says 'Over Yonder'?"

"How does it begin?" I asked, turning to the hymnbook index.

"By His great grace He will lead us to the kingdom of heaven over yonder," she replied. It was touching, for this sixth grade girl's mother had been imprisoned for selling marijuana, and her uncle's life had been taken by another person in the distant city, where he lived to work.

"What are you going to do with this hymn?" I asked the girl.

"At this time, Nkosazana, I <u>love</u> it!" she replied softly.

Escape Chief and Phumuzile came to sell a chicken for some shillings. We bought the chicken, but they received something much more valuable than shillings – eternal life! "Forgive all my sins I've done in the world," prayed Escape. "And those that I've forgotten," added another child, praying the same way one day.

In Roma's eighth grade Bible class was a boy named Philani. When he learned the way to heaven, he received Christ as his Saviour. His father had asked us to please help his boy, as he had sent him to our mission school so he would be respectful. Philani said he had been baptized, but did not know what it meant. The way of salvation was not taught where he went to church.

One day, "Found" received the Lord before setting out

to hunt for firewood for us. After he left, a knock came at our door. Two little children stood, holding a rooster they wanted to sell. We bought the chicken, and helped them to receive Christ, too.

Anna Thorntree received Christ as her Saviour. She prayed, "… Save me so when the last day comes on earth, I can go to be with Thee."

Because the other classes were preparing a program, I took an extra Sunday School class of children who had come for the first time. Three were little boys who came when they heard the early 7:30 a.m. bell for morning prayer meeting.

"Little Calabash" and Anna Thorntree (R)

"Caused–To–Be–Enlightened" came, who was in the Friday Bible class. She had a monkey–orange tucked under her dress (bulging out above her belt) – maybe for a little extra energy to get back to her kraal, three miles away. She was an excellent reader, so I gave her the Bible to read about David and Goliath. After reading for a while, she would stop and ask a question. If the answer was not given correctly, she herself, gave the right answer.

Margaret, Gift, Trust–In–The–Lord, Maggie and Nomusa went to invite Msuthu (a 12-year-old girl) to Sunday School. On the way there and back, we guessed Bible characters. The Lord helped Msuthu to receive Him. I told about the man converted in Viet Nam, who longed so to worship with other believers that to reach the closest church, he started early Saturday morning and reached home again Monday in the evening. He could have been hoeing his fields Saturday and Monday, like the unbelievers were doing. Maggie was touched. She said she was going to stop for Msuthu for Sunday School.

Msuthu came to Sunday School with Maggie. It was her first time to come. She was shy, but very happy since her conversion. Her father was in the hospital with tuberculosis.

Mrs. Laughter and others from church went with us to visit Msuthu's mother. The mother was drunk the first time we had visited her, but this time after God's word was read, she rose and said, "I choose the Lord!"

"Now, Friends of God," said Mrs. Laughter, "the child stood up the first day, and today the mother stood up. The daughters of the King came from another country. The word of Jesus was understood."

"I confessed Him a long time ago, Friends of Jesus," said Msuthu's father, who had just returned from the hospital. How we rejoiced!

One of the Durban missionaries brought us a phonograph and records from Gospel Recordings, a Christian mission. The children loved to listen to the records. The phonograph stopped if the crank was not turned, but they never tired of cranking it. They came before school, at noon, and after school to listen to the records. A boy borrowed the phonograph one noon, saying, "Now, I will hear about Jesus!"

Goodness playing gospel records for Bellina Laughter, Melta String and Salina.

Every day many bat wings fluttered in our attic at 5 p.m. The bats swarmed out in four droves through a hole near the roof, and returned by the hundreds in the mornings. Above the ceiling they scampered, tiptoed, marched, and one made a very loud thumping sound. One evening, one came down and swooped around in the room where we were. After aiming at the deftly dodging bat for quite some time with several objects, we finally brought the flier to a halt with a very wide cookie sheet. The government Department of Health exterminated the bats.

Many people were gathered at the little trading store some miles from Ekuseni. Hyenas were also known to come to the store. We bought Swiss chard and cabbage sold there by a Christian African, who came from near a river with a good water supply. It was the day the government gave pension money to elderly Zulus who were unable to work. We distributed Zulu "Way of Salvation" leaflets. A man, seated in a circle of people around a beer pot, took his leaflet and started to sing lustily (with quite a nice tune) the words we had mentioned as the leaflets were handed to them. "Read the papers carefully!" he sang.

"What is it?" asked an old man in another group.

"It tells us the way to heaven by receiving Jesus as our Saviour!" we said.

"Oh, yes!" agreed a lady who came to listen. Their eyes were weak from absorbing smoke in windowless huts, and many had missing teeth. I often missed ice cream, but on hearing and seeing this, the deprivation was worth it. It was such a joy to be there to tell them the good news of salvation!

The Lord helped Nicolina "Person–In–Want" to receive Him. "My home is right over there (beyond a donkey)," she said. "You can come and visit me," she added. We talked of the eternal home she now had. "Yes, I know I have a much better home in heaven!" she said. "You–All–Admire–Him" Majola had a knobkerrie. I asked whether he had received Christ as his Saviour. He replied, "Yes, my child. Jesus is our Great, Great One. God is watching over us!"

Children gathered around and listened eagerly to the gospel. One little girl received the Saviour that afternoon. She had left her home and come to Ekuseni. Her parents lived in different places, and had abandoned their children. One day, she had hidden under our house (which was propped up with high concrete blocks at the corners and at places underneath), begging to stay with us – when Moses (a schoolboy) tried to help her go to someone she knew.

"Where are you going?" I asked.

"I'm not going to any place!" she replied, with a determined smile.

Lydia, a schoolgirl, earned her school fees by building fires in our stove, and doing other things to set us free to work for the Lord. Her home was a long distance away, so she stayed at Ekuseni. Her father was a faithful preacher.

"My stomach has been attacking me with pain," announced a boy, arriving at the clinic. "It has been for a long time!" he added. He found rest for it, and also for his soul. Faithful "Live Ye" and another child received the Lord, too, when Roma talked with them in the clinic.

"She says she has come from a long ways," announced Lydia, reporting that a mother was waiting at the clinic with a sick baby – just as we were sitting down to eat, a little after 1 p.m. It was Tuesday, the day the dispensary was closed. But the heart of the Christian is not closed.

Someone who had been in the hospital with tuberculosis two years before held out a little, round pillbox with four green pills left in it. "It was full!" he exclaimed, indicating he wanted a refill.

A witch doctor came,

Woman (at left) wearing small horn to hold medicine a witch doctor might give.

asking for medicine for her baby, who was too heavy to carry. The baby's illness sounded like either pneumonia or whooping cough.

A young man, whom we knew was feebleminded, was brought on a sled pulled by donkeys. He arrived just too late for the district surgeon, who had already left. The family had to hire the donkeys to bring him, and could not come any sooner. So we took him to Mosvold Mission Hospital. His neck was rigid from tetanus. His mouth was open, and his head was bent backwards. He had a severe burn on his leg. He continued to live only three days at the hospital. Roma and I thought of 1 Thessalonians 5:14 – "… comfort the feebleminded …" – because that was about all we could do.

A woman from an unhappy home drank from a toxic cattle dip. We were able to help her. We hoped they would come to the Lord.

A boy was brought whose leg had been gored by a cow. He became able to walk up with his graduating class on the last day of school, with not much more than a big limp.

It was common for brothers to take turns being herdboys, so they could go to school. One went to school one year, while the other herded the cattle. Through the years, they traded places.

Paul Corner, in third grade, came to the Lord. Roma bandaged his left hand. He hurt his hand when chopping off small tree branches with a bush knife, to build fires for cooking. He prayed, "I have heard Thou hast said, 'him that cometh to me I will in no wise

Paul Corner.

cast out.' I am receiving Thee this day of today."

Jeffrey got tree poison in his eye. There was a certain tree which bothered the eyes of the one chopping it. Some sap got in his eye, but it was soon all right.

A mother came with a small elbow wound from a cow gore, with the possibility of her arm being broken. When she reached the store about four miles from Ekuseni, she found a schoolgirl ("We–Have–Been–Given–Her" Buffalo), whom she brought along as she did not know the way to our clinic.

A little girl arrived at suppertime to get some postage, reporting that as she was swinging her hand, a twenty-cent piece she was carrying flew out in the sand. Roma went with her to search for it, while I got supper. The coin was too deep in the sand to find.

Roma bound a baby's arm, and dressed a nine-year-old child's scalp wound, made by a cow's hoof. It was wonderful how the Lord helped Roma know just what to do for injuries.

Our house was made of thick asbestos wall siding. One night, half a sheet of wall siding fell down, exposing us to the outdoors. A swarm of bees came flying in! Their stings produced a hot rash and numb ears. It was a blessing the bees did not go into Roma's room. She kindly went clear down to the clinic, and got antihistamine pills and calamine lotion, which quickly extinguished the rash's fire. I had asked if I could find the medicines, but Roma said she knew "right where they were!" When we sprayed the room the next morning, all the bees became corpses, except for ten under the covers – but they moved very slowly and not for long. DDT powder was put under the corner of the house under my room, where the bees were swarming. We laughed, because we each had an itchy, hard lump in the same place on our foreheads. We got each stinger out by scraping with a sharp knife, before much poison entered.

The mother came whom we had taken up to Mosvold Mission Hospital just in time for the arrival of her baby. We had not been able to talk with her then, but later, she came to the Lord! We asked, "Who is in your heart?" The mother replied,

"Jesus." When asked, "What else do you have?" She said, smiling, "Eternal life." She named the baby "Look–To–The–Lord."

The Lord provided a Datsun pickup to gather branches for fire in the stove, and to take people to Bible conferences and the hospital. This photo shows what we had in the Datsun (from front to back) one day. At the left were large burlap sacks (brown sugar came in), full of sand for ballast. We also had a branch to probe mud holes in ruts, to see whether to go around them, out in the grass, if they were too deep. The roll of chicken wire was used to fasten around circular water-collecting tanks, before they were plastered with cement to stop up holes where water would leak out. Against the chicken wire was one page of concordance words. Behind that there was a stick to measure mud holes' depth. In my hand was a small box of alphabetized concordance words on slips of paper.

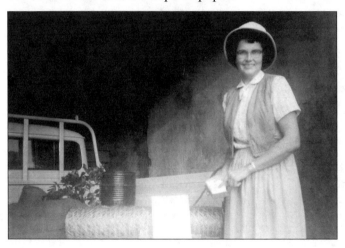

Datsun pickup.

We were thankful for our stove, even though the damper did not function, and there was a crack in the oven's floor.

Isaac's children loved to ride in the pickup, and were an excellent help. We drove to where Moses had piled up heaps of large, dead branches by the road. We brought the branches in – what a help this was in keeping the stove fire going. It took Moses so long if he did it alone. The wheelbarrow was hard to push through the sand. Moses had to go a long ways to find wood. We would run out of it before he got back if he worked alone. So the pickup was a great blessing, and we thanked the Lord for it.

We cooked twice as much on Saturday night. Then we just reheated the food on a kerosene stove on Sunday, to have a day of rest.

"Does it enter, Nkosazana?" marveled Lydia, who had just started a fire in the stove. I was blinking away tears from potent smoke, which filled the kitchen. She thought glasses would keep the smoke out! So I showed her the spaces at the sides of the bifocals. Zulus called a person who wore glasses "Four Eyes."

As we washed the dishes and clinic medicine bottles, I told Lydia about my baby nephew, David. "Is that the David you built the sweater for? Has he gotten it yet?" she asked. I had knitted a wool one for him. I smiled at her use of the word "built."

Bulky lumps formed in brown sugar stored in a large wooden bin. We set a slice of bread on top of the sugar. Soon, the brown sugar became soft and crumbly again. So that we could use cornmeal to make porridge, we scattered it out a little at a time, and removed small, red worms from it.

The ground was mostly sand. Shoe heels did not wear down, for sand is soft. This sand was about sixteen inches deep. We let air out of the pickup's tires, so they could skim over the sand – like camels' wide feet do. We headed for any tuft of grass where the sand was firmer to hold up the pickup. Even then, we could get stuck. But kind children would come running to push us right on. When we got out to the firm road, we pumped up the tires again.

We were four miles from the Indian Ocean. But we never went there, because the Zulus said there was quicksand there. We knew quicksand pulls a person down and swallows him! 1 Corinthians 6:19–20 says, "What? know ye not that your body is the temple of the Holy Ghost which is in you, which ye have of God, and ye are not your own? For ye are bought with a price: therefore glorify God in your body, and in your spirit, which are God's." We wanted to keep strong and free to work for the Lord.

We rejoiced because a fifth grade boy (who, together with his family, was an ardent Jehovah's Witness) asked for another copy of "How Jehovah's Witnesses Have Gone Astray." He had taken a copy home, and someone had asked to have it. So he needed another one!

"I am asking for Ubaqa," (a Zulu Sunday School paper) came the voice of "Strength–Of–The–Lord" Foot. His head was just visible above a water myrtle tree branch. Two thumps on the ground followed, as two small boys descended from their feast of wild fruit. "Awaken–The–Kraal" wants one, too!" he added, indicating his friend. They were happy to have two of the Zulu tracts "Jesus is Coming," which I was taking to give to people waiting at the bus stop by the road.

It was a blessing to have Lydia and Christine, two Swaziland missionaries, come for a visit. They were with us the day we reached Mkuze at noontime. While waiting for the store to open to get cement to smear around the outsides of our water tanks, we went down by the Mkuze River, and enjoyed the lunch Christine had packed for us. We were under the shade of a bush tree. We did not go close to the river. Crocodiles there came up on the banks and were carnivorous – like lions. At times, they came up to get their lunch, too. Lydia saw something moving. It was a black mamba. Black mambas can be eighteen feet long. Their bite is often fatal, causing death in five minutes. They can lift their heads very high, and glide along with great speed. It was said they could go right over a car, and even be coiled under a car – so it was wise to look carefully when getting out of a car.

There were snakes in Swaziland, too. A spitting cobra makes a hood by moving its front ribs to expand the skin of its neck. Cobras aim for a victim's eyes to defend themselves when startled. When "Looking–For–That–Blessed–Hope" (the son of Aaron, a Mhlosheni teacher) was playing in the grass, a cobra's venom entered his eyes. We put milk in the child's eyes right away. We knew it felt like gravel, but the milk neutralized the poison, and his eyes healed.

There was a retaining wall behind our house there on the mountain, to keep the walls of the house from cracking. One day, going up behind the house, I decided to take a short cut. As I stepped up onto the retaining wall, something dark flew up at the left, about three feet away, and began swaying back and forth. It was a spitting cobra. I could see its tongue rapidly flipping in and out. The Lord helped me to calmly back away, and the snake disappeared in the hedge.

Children like these played with "Looking–For–That–Blessed–Hope."

An encouraging letter came from Enid McKenzie, who was in charge of the Light of Life Bible Correspondence Courses. She wrote that she trusted we were together experiencing much joy and blessing from the Lord in our ministry, "in that dark, dark area." A letter from Maria Nilsen, who wrote the book *Malla Moe,* said:

> *You are to continue on the Concordance, I hear. I hope you get some help down there in the Bush. They say that some of the strongest evangelists have come from the Bushveld … .*

At a prayer meeting, Isaac (the preacher) read, "For the Son of man is come to seek and to save that which was lost" (Luke 19:10). Isaac said, "We used to worship snakes, idols, rivers and cows. Jesus arrived and opened the way to return Home. Jesus was seeking Zaccheus, and Zaccheus was seeking Him. They met together in their seeking. When Jesus found the lost one, He set him free! Zaccheus began to abide with Jesus. The arrival (birth) of Jesus does not end there; it continues with His return. He is power to those who lack strength in the work of the Lord. A slave does not have an inheritance, but a son does. We are His own children. 'If the Son therefore shall make you free, ye shall be free indeed' " (John 8:36). Another preacher, Philemon, came for evangelistic meetings. Speaking of sleep, Philemon mentioned God needs to "sew us up at night," as we are quite active and "come apart" in the daytime. Philemon told us the Lord delivered him when he was suddenly attacked by a mamba in the bush. His two faithful dogs, which were especially dear to him, did not survive the battle.

Wild pigs are ferocious. Isaac told us one grabbed his trouser leg and shook and shook it. But the Lord helped him get away. Shongwe fell on a bush knife when frightened by a wild pig. His hand bled as if an artery were severed. It was a blessing it was his left hand.

Mr. Mousebird earned his living by selling snakes. If he saw a snake's track in the sand, he could tell what kind it was, and the direction it had moved in. His neighbors would get word to him when a snake was seen. He managed to place the small, forked end of a long, wooden stick just behind its head, and put the snake in a wooden box he had made.

Mr. Mousebird sent live pythons and other snakes to the Durban Snake Park, and was paid so much a foot for them – sometimes earning over $1.50. One day, Roma and I were going to Durban for supplies. Mr. Mousebird brought two snakes in a wooden box for us to take to the snake park to sell for him. We put two sacks filled with sand into the pickup for ballast, and began our 100-mile trip to Durban.

As we bumped over deep corrugations in the road, three pretty, gray monkeys ran across the road in front of us. They scurried up into a tree, and gazed at us as we crawled by at 15 miles per hour – getting 35 miles to the gallon of South Africa's $4.00 a gallon petrol (gas).

Part of the way the road was just huge rocks. The vehicle

shook so violently, it seemed like all the bolts would wiggle loose, and the pickup would fall apart. We hoped the snakes' homemade box would not break open! We were thankful the ventilation holes made in it were small. The Lord helped the pickup to arrive in one piece. The keeper of the snake park invited us in to see the exhibits. He said one of the snakes we brought was a yellow Egyptian cobra.

Mr. Mousebird was a wonderful help in removing snakes. But best of all, he was an earnest preacher of the gospel – warning against "… that old serpent, which is the Devil …" (Revelation 20:2).

Charles and Beverly Smith had a snake in their kitchen at the Mangwazana Mission Station. Snakes lived under our house. A cobra killed all the little chickens under there. Older chickens, too, were taken by snakes – even in the daytime. Chickens showed no resistance. They seemed paralyzed by fright if a snake approached – which reminds us of James 4:7 – "… Resist the devil, and he will flee from you."

One of the girls, "Overcome," told us one day she heard a noise behind a cardboard box. She went over to see what it was. "And then," she said, "I saw the heap of snake!" The heap was one huge, coiled snake.

Another day, Maggie, a schoolgirl, was washing mud off the pickup's windshield, and came in to say there was a large puff adder (hognose snake) lying quietly in the garage. Puff adders are fat and sluggish, but poisonous. So a little army of about ten girls with long sticks joined us. We backed the pickup out of the way, and asked the Lord to help us to not get hurt. As the sticks struck, the puff adder immediately became unconscious. We thanked the Lord for His care. Puff adders' venom causes the skin of victims to slough off.

One day, when Elsa and I were at Esinceni to go to the Place Far Out, Mvana ("Little Lamb") came riding up on his donkey. The boy had been rolling out his grass mat in the dark to go to bed, when a puff adder bit him. His leg, which he stretched out on a wooden bench, was so swollen that the snakebite serum

Elsa (a nurse) injected oozed right out again. But when she held cotton tightly against it, the serum stayed in. After a time, the boy rode off, with his leg up on the donkey's mane. The Lord made Mvana completely well – much to the joy of us all.

Three mambas were found in our storeroom at different times. A large, green snake was seen where we got water. A little, green one did not appear again on the porch, after we boarded up the hole in the floor. Moses fixed the front door screen, so green mambas could not come in. Both black and green mambas are poisonous.

Many children came to cut grass to earn clothing. Short grass kept the snake population low.

When an evangelist was speaking, he said, "A dog does not drink beer. Why do you say it is food?" Mr. Mathenjwa spoke on Romans 12:1–2, which fitted the main need of the people so wonderfully. He also spoke on Colossians 3:22–24 which, in Zulu, ends "... serve ye the Lord Christ." He started by saying we had to excuse him – he never got to go to study the Bible. Which reminds us of 1 John 2:27 – "But the anointing which ye have received of him abideth in you, and ye need not that any man teach you ..." and of Mark 14:8 (when the Lord spoke of another who honored Him) – "She hath done what she could ...".

"Has the iron cried?" people asked, to find out whether the church "bell" had sounded – for to "ring" it, the people struck a large, iron piece hanging in a tree to invite people to come.

Mrs. Mousebird said

(L-R) Mrs. Mousebird, Mrs. Mngomezulu, Mrs. Laughter, and the converted witch doctor going to visit kraals with us.

when the church bell rang before she came to know the Lord: "I sat like a sack of cement. I was bound by chains and did not know how to break them." One day, returning home, she got to the middle of a river. She was so drunk she did not know which side to go to, to reach home. She managed to hold her baby up, so it would not drown. She decided if the Lord showed her the way to go, she would come to Him. He showed her, and she received Him. She and other Christians loved to visit in the kraals with us.

"We are going hunting for those who will be like us," said Kalina one day, asking the Lord to help us. She had found some children to guard her cornfield from monkeys, so she could go.

Auntie Marie said, "Though we are not very well in body, yet we are well in soul. We are thankful to have gotten up from our mats this morning."

"There is no other food for the journey better than the word of God!" said Mrs. Laughter.

Bushes hid the view in all directions. But we could find the way home, going toward the tall gum trees at Ekuseni. The gum trees grew from seeds a missionary planted.

We only went visiting early in the mornings. We stayed at home at noon, as it was too hot to be safe in the sun. One day, it was 104° Fahrenheit in the dark center of our home. On washday, clothes hung outdoors dried almost immediately. On humid days, paper stuck to our damp arms when we wrote letters.

We sat down on one kraaling trip in a hut of an old man who had come to Christ two months before. Plump bedbugs were crawling on the soot-blackened walls, so we slid closer to the center of the hut. Someone read, "The Lord is good, a stronghold in the day of trouble; and he knoweth them that trust in him."

"Really, I hear this!" said the old man in response. "I cried to Jehovah. I said, 'Jesus will find me.'"

Kalina turned to "Sought–For," the man's wife, earnestly urging her to come to the Saviour. "Your husband has opened the way," she explained simply. "But you reach a goal like a tortoise. Others say their husbands will not allow them to be Christians, but you have no excuse."

"I choose the Lord!" exclaimed "Sought–For," raising her hand as they do.

Cockroaches continued their swift, noiseless trips across the dirt floor. Old clumps of soot still hung thickly from ears of dried corn, suspended from a horizontal stick in the center of the ceiling above the fire pit – and the whole, dried chicken still hung beside them, but in the hearts of the living souls gathered in that simple home, there was a great, new joy that day.

"God gave Himself for us. It is fitting that a person give himself to God!" exclaimed the old man. He mentioned someone put witchcraft medicine at his hut door once. It made him sick – but God delivered him.

We went to the Mousebirds' kraal, as Mrs. Mousebird was sick. Their blanket had been stolen. Their cows had strayed off hunting for water – two had not been found yet.

Grandmother Nxumalo was tall, so she used a long cane. She thanked the Lord He enabled her to get up that morning, praying, "For it is a great work to rise – there are those to the four winds who didn't rise this morning – and to be able to tread upon Thy earth; even though the possessions disappeared seeking water, and Thy birds are thirsty, lacking dewdrops."

Mrs. Mousebird said, "What can we say? Let us return to Jesus. He is our fortress. His yoke is lighter than the yokes of earth. Jesus is our shelter, People of God!"

We met a girl who listened to the gospel with such a thankful face. She said, "We are overcome by that," as she pointed to a foaming beer pot.

"No one can save us. Do you know who? What can we do?" asked another Zulu. It was a joy to give the precious gospel answer!

A grandmother, Evelina, was a witch doctor, but the Lord transformed her into such a faithful Christian. It was so touching to hear her pray for "the daughters of the King who live amongst us sinners," for we know "… there is no difference: For all have sinned, and come short of the glory of God" (Romans 3:22–23). How thankful we are that when we ask the Lord to forgive our sins and come in and be our Saviour, we are "… justified freely by his grace through the redemption that is in Christ Jesus" (Romans 3:24).

One day, a Christian girl with a knife wound in her head fled into our home, and hid behind clothes hanging in a closet. The person seeking to take her life soon reached our porch. At first, he said his heart was so black, he would wait until the next day to listen to us. But the word of God is so powerful. To hear that we loved him and longed for him to be in heaven with us, too, and especially "and ye know that no murderer hath eternal life abiding in him …" (1 John 3:15) touched his heart. We thanked the Lord – for it was a marvelous deliverance, for which we praised Him so very, very much. "… God hath power to help …" (2 Chronicles 25:8).

We took offerings to a blind grandfather, who had been enabled to escape out of his hut one night, as it burned with all his belongings. On the way, Mrs. Mngomezulu exclaimed, "God has power!" as she pointed to the very two who had run to our home so unhappily a few days before. The girl who had fled for a place of refuge, and the one who had listened to the powerful word of God, were sitting together peacefully, under a shade tree in their kraal, some distance from our path!

Along the way, we met a man carrying a bucket who stopped his bicycle to greet us. We asked him, "Do you know the way to heaven?" He replied, "No, I am the one who needs to find it!" Which he did.

At unbelieving "Come–To–Nought's" kraal, Mrs. Laughter said to the people, "Jesus died for all. He didn't choose the color of people. You see these white ones come into the hut and sit on the ground. Other white people stand out in the yard, and call us to come to work. These here bring you out of darkness. Others don't do that. The name of Jesus is a fortress. We long to patch ourselves with Jesus. We need to be built up in love – and you, my girls who've just come in," she added, as two more girls from the kraal just arrived.

We found Christians at Put's kraal. "Come, my people!" called Grandfather Put, inviting us in.

"How are you?" asked Grandmother.

"We have lived!" replied the converted witch doctor with us. "We were full of mud and dressed in rags – poor, destitute people. We were a thing – animals! If we stick tight to Jesus, we have everlasting life."

"I was born in Cetshwayo's time, when there was darkness," said Grandfather (who must have been about 100 years old); "and today, darkness doesn't want to leave us. When you lift up for me the waterpot from the one fountain where Jesus is, you are my friends!"

"Oh, Friends of God," said Mrs. Mousebird, "we are thankful to hear you drink from the same Fountain we do!"

When we got back home, Evelina prayed before we all separated, "Though we did not get any deer – as Thy word says we should bring in the lost – yet where we went, Thou canst still speak." It is true, indeed, that His word does not return void.

One day, we reached the kraal of Mrs. Magagula, a witch doctor. She said, "Sometimes I wonder where I am going to go (eternally)!" We read in Deuteronomy 18 that a witch is an abomination to the Lord, and in Revelation 21 that the abominable have their part in the lake of fire. She was touched to see the joy of the Lord in Evelina, for she knew Evelina used to be a witch doctor.

We stopped to visit two mothers who had received the Lord, but had not been with us at church. Evelina suggested going to see them. She knew them, and was longing that they be with us. The older mother said she wanted to come, but demons kept her from it. The younger one said she wanted to come, too. So after we had read Hebrews 10:25 – "Not forsaking the assembling of ourselves together, …" Evelina spoke wonderfully of how the Lord had delivered her from demons, mentioning that He is stronger than Satan (1 John 4:4). And the mothers said they planned to come! Mrs. Mousebird asked for the verse in Hebrews, pulling out a little piece of paper from her pocket to write on. (There were two at her kraal who could read.) "I want to learn it!" she said.

"Are you still in good health?" asked the grandmother at a kraal we reached. "We are still slightly in good health. We are walking with a cough," she added. They often say they are not quite well, so that evil spirits will not make them sick.

"The daughters of the King have come so a person can be an heir of heaven, instead of an heir of the world," explained Mrs. Laughter.

As we passed a herd of cattle, a young ox shook his horns back and forth at us. The ladies in front retreated a little, and got some sticks. Then the ox became docile.

Along our way, we saw a large, mud nest in a tree. Mrs. Laughter said it was the home of fierce, brown ants. When we came to a locust tree, she warned about its thorns when I stopped to pick a blossom. "That's all right," she said. "The flowers don't have thorns – it's their mother. She doesn't want people to pick her children."

We passed plants, where tall, glass bottles with broken off tops were collecting sap to make beer.

Tall bottle to collect sap (at left).

At one kraal, we found an old man with a braided beard, making a basket. The Lord helped three schoolgirls to come to Him there. Roma gave them each a Gospel of John.

There were fifteen children at the next kraal. "Caused–To–Be–Enlightened," from Friday's Bible class, was pleased we recognized her. Mrs. Laughter told them not to be discouraged and not to complain – like the Israelites did in the wilderness with Moses – even though it may be difficult to live here. She mentioned these white ones who had come to them on such a hot day, when "other people who are white like them are sitting in the shade, drinking cold lemonade. And tonight, they will be hurt by their heads" (Zulu for 'have headaches') "from walking in the hot sun."

Masikela sent for us. His mother was dying. Going along with some of the church ladies, we met people munching on sweet potatoes as they planted groundnuts. They showed us the way to Masikela's. His mother could no longer hear. Someone voiced what Masikela was now realizing – that this visit was for him, as it was too late for his mother to understand. Mary, one of us, mentioned preparing to meet the Lord. "My daughter and I were talking about it just this morning," she said. "How shall we escape if we neglect so great salvation! Don't waste this opportunity, which is so very important!"

"I choose the Lord!" declared Masikela.

"I hear the angels beating their wings!" exclaimed Mary, her face beaming. There was great rejoicing in the little hut.

At the next kraal, when we told them about Masikela, the father there said, "I told them to send for the Christians." The next day, a child brought word Masikela's mother had died. While we were there, an eleven-year-old boy received Christ.

The Zulus belong to a family of peoples called "Bantu," which means "People." One day, going to kraals, we saw the farm of some white people on a far mountain.

"What is their surname?" I asked.

"Oh, they're not People! They don't have a surname," one of our Zulu companions replied!

I mentioned to Maggie, an excellent Zulu Concordance helper, that I had seen a man in Durban, who translated the Bible into Zulu.

Maggie helping make the concordance.

"Was he a Person?" she asked excitedly.

"No, but the People marveled so, because he <u>talked</u> just like a Person," I replied.

One day, Maggie had some candy corn. "If I plant it, will it grow?" she asked. "No," I explained with a smile; "it will not grow." It would not have to be ground between two stones, or cooked, either!

A blind grandfather was the first man in the area to allow his daughter to go to school. Others did not believe in girls being educated. When his daughter was in school, all the other students were boys.

Trains were slow. A man shipped something by train from Durban to Pongola. Then he walked the 232 miles, and reached Pongola before the train did.

One day, a pigeon landed on the edge of our roof. It did not move when we approached it, so we reached up and took it. We noticed a band on its leg, which revealed it was from Portugal. The park ranger was happy to hear about it.

The water in St. Lucia Bay was very, very blue. In their

season, flamingoes made the area pink. The word for yellow in Zulu is "yolk of egg."

One beautiful sunset, at Ekuseni, was all pink with a bright, shining evening star and slim crescent moon. Two gray monkeys slipped across the road.

Driving along the Hluhlue Game Reserve, we saw beautiful zebras and wildebeest. We had heard that a rhinoceros once went berserk there, and crashed its big horn into the tourist cabins. We saw a rhinoceros in the distance, and got out of our pickup to get a little closer view of the amazing animal. Then it spotted us, and started in our direction! We quickly turned toward our vehicle. The Lord helped us pick up speed before the rhinoceros did. We left in a hurry. Further along the way, a football-sized turtle, starting across the road, pulled its head in, and waited until we passed. Five impala were nearby. All but one gracefully bounded across in front of us.

One day, when we were back at home again, we decided to go out to the road and fill in the deep, wide ruts which had been made by sleds hauling heavy drums of water. Then the pickup would not bounce so hard. While we were working on this, a man came by with his oxen, greeted us happily, and said, "My smaller wife is sick." Noting our surprise, he quickly added, "I took the two wives before I got salvation!"

One day, two children came and asked for the brown leaves at the base of our aloe plants to use for tobacco. So we mentioned, "Abstain from all appearance of evil" (1 Thessalonians 5:22) and 1 Corinthians 3:16–17 and 6:19–20. After they left, Roma and I realized we needed to get rid of the aloes. We felt it would be wise to remove them at night, when not being noticed. There was plenty of bougainvillea growing, which was prettier, anyway.

When there was a full moon, we went out and chopped down the eighteen big aloe plants. We took them down to a pit by wheelbarrow, and chopped off the big, succulent leaves. "Awuzwake!" we exclaimed to the aloes. We had once heard a little girl cry out, "Awuzwake!" ("Just feel that!") when a trouble–making snake was being destroyed. We felt the same way as we chopped the leaves off. No one objected – probably all the people were asleep, anyway. The ones who liked the aloes did not live close by. It was better to dispose of them at night, as those who liked them might be close in the daytime – and might not approve too heartily.

Mr. Vick, of Scripture Gift Mission, sent us English questions to be translated into Zulu, so schoolchildren could earn Zulu New Testaments and Bibles by answering the questions. We translated the questions and returned them. Then he sent us printed copies. Eighty-three children took questions to answer. To earn a notebook for answering the questions, "Look–At–Him" Chief shelled peanuts. When he tried to erase an answer he had written, it did not rub off very well – for his "eraser" was a little, flat, hard piece of tire inner tube. We gave him a better eraser.

Isaiah, a sixth grade boy, earned a Zulu New Testament by answering a question in each chapter of the New Testament. Mr. Mousebird came by just then, and was delighted Isaiah had earned the New Testament. He prayed the Lord would help Isaiah to grow and become a preacher of the gospel – "for it needs those who will be its preachers."

Alphaeus taught school in the mountains, forty-five miles farther north. He returned home for vacation, and was so happy to hear about the Bible Searching questions. He took the Johannesburg Scripture Gift Mission address, so he could send for questions, and his pupils could earn Zulu Bibles.

A student wrote this letter to thank the Scripture Gift Mission:

My Friends,

I am greeting you in the name of our Lord Jesus Christ. In writing this letter, I take away the debt of thanking for your cause, kindness and love of giving us the Holy Bible questions of the New Testament so that we can earn a certificate and the gift of the New Testament.

My Friends, I thank the kindness of our Father in heaven,

who has given me the power, and the longsuffering and the love to answer the questions with patience, even though some overcame me. I asked from Jesus that He help me to see. Now I have succeeded ... As for me, who write here, I am a child who studied eighth grade last year, but this year I did not go to take Form I. If the Lord has appointed me, I will go this year which is coming. I have fifteen years. I have my verse here which I am liking. It says: "Even though I walk in the valley of the shadow of death, I will not be afraid of evil because Thou art with me. Thy fighting-stick and Thy walking-staff are comforting me." We find it in the hymn of David – PSALM 23:4.

Pardon about the mistakes and bad handwriting.

It is I, who humbles herself in the Lord,

Siphiwe Buffalo

People came continually to get water from our deep well. The Lord made very tall, strong grass grow there. "Live Ye" made a belt with one blade of grass.

Zulus made long, braided-grass ropes to let their gallon dipping buckets down into the well. In the dry season, people waited patiently all night long, for a little more water to seep back into the well. We could hear their buckets. They emptied the water into large drums, which oxen pulled home on forked tree branches.

The name of one boy, who brought oxen to haul water home was "You Hit

Drums around the well.
Tall gum trees (in background).

Him." Children, whose parents did not know the Lord yet, had similar, unusual names.

One day, a government truck came. It was like our long, cylindrical vehicles in America, which haul gas. It was full of water. They drove all around in Zululand to fill wells. What a blessing! Jesus said in John 4:14 – "But whosoever drinketh of the water that I shall give him shall never thirst …".

Surplus deer were culled in the game park. Two deer were sent to Ekuseni School, and the children had a happy feast! This reminds us Jesus said, "… I am the bread of life: he that cometh to me shall never hunger; and he that believeth on me shall never thirst" (John 6:35).

Bazwani Whirlpool, a schoolboy, came to the Lord on hearing 1 John 5:11–13.

"What do you have now?" I asked.

"Eternal life!" he said.

"Where?" I asked – expecting him to say, "In heaven."

He gave a beautiful answer, "In the hand of Jesus!" It was just what Jesus said in John 10:28 – "And I give unto them eternal life: and they shall never perish, neither shall any man pluck them out of my hand."

Chapter 11

Zulu Bible Concordance

"**D**on't you think we should have a verse to go with it?" asked one of seven missionary children, when they came to play a game someone had sent. Their question brought to mind Colossians 3:16 – "Let the word of Christ dwell in you richly …". They listened earnestly while John 11:1-36 was read.

A concordance is considered to be the most valuable of all references for Bible study. George Truett, in his book, *A Quest for Souls* tells that when Charles ("Chinese") Gordon went into the Sudan, taking his splendid library, he soon found he really needed only two books: the Bible, and a Bible concordance. When Dwight L. Moody was a new Christian, he searched for days trying to find a Scripture passage to help a young convert, whom a skeptic was trying to lead astray. Later, Moody learned that if he had had a concordance, he could have found the passage in a few moments. Charles Spurgeon wrote on the flyleaf of his concordance in January, 1869: "For these 10 years, this has been the book at my left hand while the Word of God has been at my right."

In about 1956, a concordance was produced for people near Burma. The thought came: "Oh, that the Zulus could have one, too!" There were so few Christian books in Zulu that they would all fit into a very small suitcase.

We began with prayer to compile the Zulu Concordance, realizing "Not that we are sufficient of ourselves to think any thing as of ourselves; but our sufficiency is of God" (2 Corinthians 3:5). I did not know how to start, or how to continue the work, but the Lord continually guided in marvelous ways. He said, "Fear thou not; for I am with thee ... for I am thy God ... I will help thee ... and thou shalt glorify me" (Isaiah 41:10, Psalm 50:15). It was impossible to translate it from English. Where the English Bible says Christ is on the right hand of God, the Zulu Bible says He is at the right side of God. The word "hand" is not there at all in Zulu.

As in Zulu dictionaries, it was necessary to alphabetize words by their stems. "Kwakungukwahlukaniselwa" (the longest word in the Zulu Bible) is not listed under its first letter, "K," but under "A." There are four "a's" in this word. The second "a" begins the stem. The Lord answered Job "out of the whirlwind" – "esesikhwishikhwishini." This word has two "k's." The first "k" begins the stem. It is necessary to know the language, to know where the stem begins.

Zulu words are interesting. The word for "raisins" is "fruits of the vine which have been dried." Solomon's throne was made of "the tusks of the elephant" (ivory). A "stammerer" is an "isingingingi" in Isaiah, describing Messiah's kingdom when stammerers can speak plainly. The Zulu word for "south" is "iningizimu" ("many cannibals" – for they were in the south). The words for "south-west" are "iningizimu engasentshonalanga" ("many cannibals at the disappearing of the sun.")

In Amos 5:21 the Lord says, "I hate, I despise your feast days ...," and that Zulu word ("imihlangano") for "feast days," is never mentioned again in the rest of the Zulu Bible.

"Pain" is mentioned fifty-five times in the Zulu Bible. The last verse where it is recorded says there will be no more pain in heaven (Revelation 21:4).

The Zulu Bible was gradually printed in the new orthography, which Zulus now use.

"May I use your big concordance?" asked Dora, a Zulu teacher. We used Strong's Concordance. Her pupils had asked whether even young children could become Christians. She found Jesus' words, "… Suffer the little children to come unto me, and forbid them not:" (Mark 10:14) and others, to show them.

"I wish the Zulu Concordance was finished!" I commented.

"I do, too!" she said. The words were so different that an English concordance was not helpful enough.

In 1958, I arranged the Mark references for the Zulu Concordance on the "African Rainbow" freighter, when returning to South Africa from New York.

The recording of the rest of the New Testament references was done at Franson Christian High School at Mhlosheni in Swaziland. We put bricks under the legs of adjacent tables, and spread out sheets of paper on the tables. Higher tables prevented

Classroom in which we worked Saturdays.
By the windows are Abraham, Daniel and Barnabas.

*Sheets of
Bible words
spread out
on tables.*

*Gloria, Mary
(in charge
of girls'
dormitory)
and Minah*

stooping, and were more comfortable for hours of writing. Pages already prepared for the concordance helped to find answers to questions.

"Where is the story of Zaccheus?" asked a seventh grade student. We looked in our "Z" pages and found it quickly.

"Where is 'Study to shew thyself approved unto God'?" asked another student.

"If a person doubts whether he is saved, and dies, then is he?" asked a high school teacher – another question to which our prepared pages helped find the answer.

"We know where it tells about different tongues (Genesis

11), but why are our skins different?" asked a sophomore girl. We found the Lord "… hath done all things well …" (Mark 7:37, Colossians 1:16).

Elias, a sophomore, needed the verse "… every idle word that men shall speak, they shall give account thereof in the day of judgment." We looked in the "judgment" phrases. "It is wonderful!" he exclaimed, when the Lord helped to quickly find the verse (Matthew 13:36).

Christine Trevvett needed a verse to go with the chorus, "Let us praise Him!" for junior chapel. We rejoiced to be able to find the very verse needed.

A former student was very discouraged. To encourage Christians, it is helpful to know that the word "coward" occurs only once in the Zulu Bible, and in a very serious place – in the list of those who "… shall have their part in the lake which burneth with fire and brimstone: which is the second death" (Revelation 21:8). The Lord helped this student to overcome an unusual disappointment, and go on faithfully for Him.

Over 100 Swazi students helping make the concordance were encouraged, too. "What verse is that – that says we are of heaven?" asked Lillian, after the reference numbers for Philippians 3:20 were recorded. She commented on another one once, too, and made lists of references of verses she liked.

"Love suffereth long," I found jotted on a sheet of cardboard, after a helper (who had come to that verse) had left for the day.

"Excuse me, Nkosazana. Are these papers going to be connected?" asked a freshman, indicating the prepared sheets. When I said we hoped to make them into a book, so needed verses could be found easily, she said, "It is good." It was encouraging to hear her say this. It had taken three years for her to pass in one grade, and if she understood it would be a help, surely others would, too.

Amongst the students who came to help after school and on Saturdays were Abraham, Joshua, Caleb, Grace, Daniel, Israel, John, Luke (whom the others affectionately called "Doctor" – as his name was like that of "the beloved physician" in the Bible),

Mary, Moses, Othniel, Rebekah, Samuel, Saul, Trust and three Ruths.

John (grandson of Johane Gamede, who went with the Gospel Wagon) and Joshua

Saul and Trust

"Is this a Bible?" Abraham asked, on seeing the large Strong's Concordance the first time he came to help – "Does it tell how many may be saved?"

We looked up "saved" and read Romans 10:13 – "For whosoever shall call upon the name of the Lord shall be saved."

"Do you know how many it is?" I asked.

"I beg your pardon?" he queried. Then I realized he had asked, "Does it tell how 'we' may be saved?"

"Yes, it shows us where to find the verses explaining salvation. Have you received Christ as your Saviour?"

"Yes!" he replied.

Abraham worked patiently on the phrases. Then one day, he went to the hospital for heart valve surgery. The doctor opened Abraham's heart, but quickly closed it again. Abraham did not come back. He went to heaven.

We missed Abraham, but rejoiced to know he had gone to be with Christ "... which is far better" (Philippians 1:23).

I learned precious lessons while working on the concordance. Darrell Jacobson, one of the missionary children at home for vacation, came to inquire about helping. We always prayed, asking the Lord to guide us, when we started working. The ten-year-old child was of great assistance that afternoon. Then the 5:30 school bell rang for supper.

(L-R) Lynn Hart, Joyce Jacobson, Ida,
Darrell Jacobson (blinking in the sun) and Cheri Hart

"I guess we'll have to stop now!" I said. When putting things away across the room, I realized Darrell was still sitting there. I glanced over – to see him looking up, questioningly.

"We haven't thanked Him!" Darrell said softly. He led us in prayer, giving thanks that the Lord had helped us, and that he could learn how to do it.

From then on, we remembered to thank the Lord at the <u>close</u> of each day, too.

"I am asking for work," said Isabel, a third-grader, shyly.

I asked her to find the book of James. She searched in the Old Testament. Then I remembered she had just come at recess time to buy a New Testament, and was probably just beginning to learn the books of the Bible. She seemed too young to be able to help yet, so I mentioned she could help better when she had grown a little more. Three days later, Isabel appeared again, intending to help! (I had had in mind more like three <u>years</u>!)

"I am asking for work!" she announced, expectantly.

Then I wondered, "Why is the Lord sending this child?" I got the Zulu Bible again, turned to a book, and asked her to find a certain chapter and verse. She found it immediately! We were only working with one book at a time! That was the beginning of many happy afternoons – with the keen, little girl finding verse after verse, so I could make phrases quickly. The older girls were working in the garden (after school) to earn their school fees. At the time when they were not available, the Lord provided this precious child!

At the end of one day, Isabel was thanking the Lord for helping us. She closed her prayer: "Sleep with Nkosazana – and take me home safely."

"Oh, Isabel! Are you going home tonight?" I asked – a bit alarmed, as it would not be wise to go to her home, some miles away in Galilee, at such a late hour.

"No," she said, and explained she was just going to the home of Mama Mathenjwa (a school cook), just a few houses away, to spend the night. Only later did I learn that she lived there when school was in session. Her prayer helped me remember to look to the Lord always – even when in safe places and pleasant surroundings.

When I showed a Zulu preacher what the concordance would be like, he asked, "When will this be ready?" I was not sure. I mentioned my mother had had an operation, and there was a need to go to America to care for her – but the Lord helped my sister leave the National League for Nursing in New York to care for our mother, and this enabled me to continue work on the concordance.

"We thank the Lord about that!" he exclaimed.

"How are you getting on with the Zulu Concordance? We'll be using it, too, when you get it published!" wrote a missionary with the Ndebele tribe, in what is now Zimbabwe. There are 10,500,000 Zulu people. Four tribes of Nguni people would be able to use the concordance. Swazi and Xhosa tribes could use it, too.

"How soon will it be printed?" asked Preacher Isaac Mkwanazi.

"When will it be finished?" asked another Zulu preacher.

"We don't care how much it costs – just so we can have it!" said a Swazi Bible teacher.

One day, when entering a hospital to visit Zulu and Xhosa patients, I noticed a cluster of visitors had already gathered around the first patient. As I slipped on past to visit others, one of the young Zulus visiting called out, "Have you finished the concordance? We're hungry!"

Preacher Isaac Mkwanazi with concordance galleys we proofread.

Someone wrote from Cape Town:

Friends of Jesus and of the Zulu nation,

The work which you are doing, do with double diligence; because it will not be in vain in the Lord Jesus. Your work of writing the concordance for us is not small at all; and one who understands the accomplishment of it can say that in heavy work like this the strength that comes from the Lord is what encourages you. We will be happy to see the concordance of the Old Testament and New Testament. When the Lord hastens the reply to our prayers, He gave you strength to complete this work, which you began by His grace.

It is I, who am just a very small one in the mercy of the Lord,

Ngidi

Three thousand New Testament concordances were printed in 1964. Proofreading its galleys was like reading the New Testament eighteen times.

A Zulu hospital chaplain was nearly in tears when he received his New Testament concordance – holding it closely under his jacket.

Charles Smith went to visit a Zulu preacher who did not seem to be at home in his kraal. Charles finally found him behind a hut, sitting on a haystack, reading the Zulu New Testament Concordance.

We began work on the entire Bible concordance in 1965. One hundred forty-six more New Testament words were included than we had listed in the New Testament Concordance already in print.

We found two pages of words from the Zulu Bible which were not listed in the Zulu dictionary.

American Christians sent clothing for those helping with the concordance. "Goodness" (one of the young helpers) sent a note, revealing how deeply it was appreciated:

Nkosazana,

I am still going to ask at home that I don't go at the end of school. I will hear from my mother what she says, because really I want to work because I am an orphan. I was bereaved of my father. I am still a child. Now I have gotten the blessing of getting clothes free, because it is just like I get them free – I don't buy them. I don't know what my mother will say. I hope she will consent. Stay with grace, Nkosazana.

It is I,

Goodness

Goodness finding Bible verses.

It was interesting to see familiar blouses, skirts and sweaters as the students returned to school, and to be reminded of the students' faithful help while earning them, and of the great wisdom we had felt all along from the Lord in arranging the words.

The girls who helped record the references were such a blessing. Word quickly spread through the bush. Soon after we returned from an annual missionary conference, Goodness and "Found" arrived to continue with the work that very afternoon! It was a surprise to see Goodness. She had finished eighth grade, and I had heard she would be leaving to attend high school quite some distance away.

"I am going to work," Goodness announced.

"Where are you going to work?" I asked.

"To you!" she continued, smiling. And I smiled, too – with

deep gratitude to God – realizing she could help all day! The other girls could only come after school during the week, and on Saturdays. Goodness' family thought she was too young to go away to school yet.

Mrs. Guthrie, a missionary in what is now Zambia, asked how we compiled the concordance. She wanted to make a Chinyanja Bible concordance. It was a joy to show her the steps the Lord guided to take. This is how we did the work: First, I underlined the words' stems in a Zulu Bible. We wrote the words on 2 by 3-inch slips of inexpensive newsprint paper, and placed them alphabetically – at first, in a small box and eventually, in a long shoebox lid. I typed these words on the backs of seventy-four mimeographed paper sheets the Lord provided from Lydia Rogalsky, who no longer needed them for her work in the mission schools. The mimeographed paper was 8½ by 13 inches.

We placed a large sheet of ceiling plasterboard on the tops of five chairs, to make a comfortable height to work without stooping. Two girls had the same name, so they named themselves Goodness I and Goodness II.

Girls carrying a chair and table for the concordance work.

We spread out the seventy-four sheets of 5,843 alphabetized Zulu words on the plasterboard "table," overlapping them as much as possible, to save space.

Beside each word, six to twelve schoolgirls at a time wrote

down the books of the Bible in which it occurred. When we came to "langazelela" in Genesis 31:30, the girl nearest the "L" words repeated "langazelela" to confirm that she heard it correctly. She then put a blue "G" by it for "Genesis." When "sabalala" was reached in Exodus, the girl nearest the "S" words put a red "E" by it for "Exodus."

(L-R) Beauty, Goodness I, Goodness II, Sheila, Found and "We–Have–Been–Given–Her."

From these seventy-four sheets, I typed a set of words for each book of the Bible, on long, yellow paper that had been around X-ray film. Peggy Wallace kindly sent these yellow sheets to us from Mosvold Mission Hospital. Psalms required thirty yellow sheets.

I typed out the Genesis words. We spread out these Genesis sheets on the "table." Each girl kept in mind the number of the chapter for which we were recording references. I read out the number of the verse followed by its word: "1 –qala (ukuqala) ('beginning')." The girl nearest the "Q" words then wrote "1:1" beside " –qala (ukuqala)." When we came to it in verse five, the girl put a comma after the last "1," and then recorded "5" (1:1, 5) (The "first" day in verse 5 in English is called the "beginning" day in Zulu.) As each chapter was finished, the girl marked it off with red.

After all the books were finished in that way, we repeated the entire process on white sheets. We compared them with the yellow sheets, and recorded any corrections on the final white sheets.

I typed the first Genesis word listed on the seventy-four sheets of alphabetized words. Under this word, I typed all the phrases listed for it on the Genesis white sheet.

To find books of the Bible easily, I fastened on each book a protruding label made from the white, gummed edge strips of South African postage stamp sheets.

When making a number of phrases from only one book of the Bible, we slipped a large envelope over the pages just preceding the book, and another envelope over the pages just after the book – so that we did not waste time searching for verses in the wrong book. The Lord continually showed us similar ways in which to make the work much easier. We sensed the faithful prayers of others on our behalf, and were so very, very thankful.

Violeria Thorntree, the smallest child in the Friday Bible class, stopped by my window with a friend, early in the mornings, to greet – and watch the typewriter.

I had purchased a light "Skywriter" typewriter in America on one furlough, so I could travel by air. By sea, it had taken one month and two ships to reach South Africa in 1951.

The very convenient, seven-pound Skywriter was a great help, until a piece of it broke off. The repairman said, "Is this used very much? It is really only to use if you go on an airplane trip!"

A kerosene lamp gave good light to make phrases in the evenings. It had no lampshade, but I wore a surplus army helmet to shade my eyes. I also painted the helmet with white shoe polish to wear during the day in the blazing sun.

It took a long time to make the phrases, but I could type them many hours a day and after supper. However, it got so that even when asleep or awake, my mind was constantly making Zulu phrases – like a robot! At a routine physical checkup, Dr. Douglas Taylor asked if I made phrases in the evenings. He mentioned some felt it was better to burn out than to rust out. "But I think there's a happy medium," he gently counseled.

The fine print of the Zulu Bible dimmed my eyesight. But on a supply trip, I found a large–print Zulu Bible, which helped.

We finished making the concordance near Johannesburg in the Word of Life Literature Centre, where there were morning chapel services and offices on the second floor. The bookstore was on the first floor. When the Israelis won the Six Days War, all the prophecy books were sold within three days.

Word of Life Literature Centre.

We used four reams of long newsprint sheets, and typed two columns of phrases on each side of a sheet. We determined the length of newsprint needed by measuring the distance from the

Mavis helping hold a long newsprint sheet.

typewriter to the floor – about one yard. We would have had to put 8½ by 11-inch papers in and out sixteen times, to make the number of phrases one long newsprint sheet held.

Joyce "Present– A–Cow– For– Slaughter" looking up Bible verses.

The Lord helped us see that additional words could be added to the phrases by using a typesetter. On a typewriter, an "i" took the same space as an "m." On a typesetter, an "i" took only one-third the space of an "m."

A typesetter is very helpful for a language with long words – such as Zulu. In Psalm 16:8 – "because he is at my right hand, I shall not be moved" reads "ngokuba ungakwesokunene sami, angiyikuzanyazanyiswa" ("I shall not be shaken").

The Lord helped to obtain a second-hand typesetter. The content of a verse could be shown much better by including key words, and using dots to exclude others. We changed the typed phrases to longer ones:

"he was warned by an angel" became "Cornelius ... was warned by an angel".

"Abraham gave him ... of it" became "Abraham gave him a tenth part".

"he dwelt in a separate house" became "the king ... dwelt in a separate house".

The typeface element was changed once in each line, to

make the first letter of the word (being listed) in bold type. This made over 510,000 changes.

By doing our own typesetting, we saved over $10,000. Mavis, a faithful Zulu helper, typeset much of the fine, 8-point print. One time, the "i" was not working well on the typesetter. At the close of the day, Mavis was thanking the Lord for helping us get so much done, "even though the 'i' is tired."

Once, we heard visitors were coming the next day. Mavis prayed to the Lord, "When they see our work, may they praise <u>Thee</u>!"

Mavis changing the typeface element.

The New Testament concordances were all sold. Then in 1978, 3,000 Zulu concordances of the entire Bible were printed. This entire Bible concordance is exhaustive. If a word is included, every place it occurs in the Bible is listed. There are about 262,000 phrases included in the 1,018 pages of the book. I thank the Lord for all the faithful Christians who helped make it. It was a blessing to have others help with the proofreading. Charles and Beverly Smith proofread 286 galleys, before opening the thriving TEAM Book Store in Empangeni. They discovered an "n" instead of an "s" in Proverbs 25:27, making it mistakenly read that it is not good to eat many "birds" (instead of much "honey"). Wesley and Norma Carlson proofread 916 galleys.

There were opportunities to explain the use of the concordance at the Transvaal Zulu Bible study workshop, at a conference of about 100 Zulu Christian workers in the chapel of the University of Zululand, and at the annual Bible conference of the Evangelical Teacher Training College in Vryheid, Natal.

"Don't you have this in Sotho?" asked someone from that language area.

Sotho family, in their cart, take a tract along an Orange Free State road.

A letter came, asking:

Do you have this in Xhosa?

"It is something wonderful for our language really!" said Mr. Vilakazi, the Swaziland Bible Society representative, at his booth near the Swaziland flag, at the Swaziland Independence celebration.

A Johannesburg Zulu preacher wrote:

I am greeting you in the name of the Lord Jesus. We are thanking you for the great, good work. With this Concordance, I have found verses I have been seeking for a long time, which I couldn't find before. I am thanking.

A Zulu man who bought a concordance liked it so much he got seventeen more, and took them to a conference. But he came back to Samuel, the Zulu Christian who sold books at the Word of Life Publishers, to get eighteen more, saying, "Oh, these are going like hotcakes!" And he thought he would be back for more.

A Swaziland store customer wanted a Zulu Bible, with a concordance in the back! The concordance is two inches thick!

I met two Zulus in the Durban Christian Book Room. On seeing the concordance, one of them said, "As for me, I work in the post office. I have seen it, but I don't have it." I showed him how to find a verse. "Oh, you have read it – you know it," he said. The other man was from the south coast. "How much is it?" he queried. He asked to have the name and price written on the paper sack containing his newly purchased Bible.

An eastern Transvaal preacher said, "The time of study of the Bible is a time which I always have a longing for, since I now know the way to use the concordance."

Swaziland evangelists said, "It is a book which has many marvels. We thank God that He would give us a book like it."

"It helps very much. It makes everything clear," said Gilbert of Durban.

Another Christian wrote:

I am thanking for the gift of God our Father in heaven Who has given strength to the makers of the concordance which helps in the study of the Holy Bible. To me this book has help in easily finding Bible verses. If I don't know in what book of the Bible a verse is found, the concordance will tell quickly – if you just know one word in it. This book is a great help to those who study the Bible in homes or no matter where they are. We must have this book, which helps us so many times in finding verses quickly.

Paul and Annette Hayward mentioned in a prayer letter that one of the greatest needs in South Africa was the reprinting of the Zulu Concordance. What a blessing it was that "Back to the Bible" and other saints of the Lord made the printing of 3,000 more possible. This helped the word of the Lord to "have free course, and be glorified ..." (2 Thessalonians 3:1).

John and Beulah, retired Iowa dairy farmers, kindly gave

a $100 bill. They did this seventeen times. Beulah only had one tooth, and could easily have had comfortable dentures. But they laid up for themselves treasures in heaven (Matthew 6:20). When they went to heaven, they left part of the sale price of their farm – and an ongoing annuity – for the work of the Lord.

Another edition may need to be printed in 2011. Eight thousand, two hundred concordances have been sold in all. There are 800 left of the second edition.

Timothy, the Zulu manager of the TEAM Bookstores' stockroom in Johannesburg wrote:

The Zulu people's greatest need has been met. In Zulu there is no Chain-Reference Bible; there is no Bible Dictionary; there is not much that is good for Bible study for a Zulu Bible student.

I have sold books at the Gold Mines, bus stations, railway stations and busy places like this. But always people asked me the same question: "When are we going to have good Zulu books – that help us with Bible study?" Their question has been answered by this Zulu concordance.

I am glad the Lord has given us Zulus a good Bible study book in our own language, because it is not every Zulu that can understand English well. In the past it meant studying both the Bible and the English language, but now we can study the Bible in our own language – Zulu.

We have got nothing to boast about, but we have something to thank the Lord for – and that is the Zulu concordance.

Jesus said, "... without me ye can do nothing" (John 15:5). Philippians 4:13 says, "I can do all things through Christ which strengtheneth me."

So we praise the Lord He has provided a way to help Zulu, and other Christians, to win souls for Him! "O Lord, my God, I will give thanks unto thee for ever" (Psalm 30:12).

If any who are not Christians yet have read this book, I trust they will repent, and ask Christ to forgive their sins and come in and be their Saviour, so they can go to heaven, and not be in the lake of fire for ever!" (Revelation 20:15). "… God hath given to us eternal life, and this life is in his Son. He that hath the Son hath life; and he that hath not the Son of God hath not life. These things have I written unto you that believe on the name of the Son of God; that ye may <u>know</u> that ye have eternal life …" (1 John 5:11–13).

POSTSCRIPT

"Awake to righteousness, and sin not; for some have not the knowledge of God: I speak this to your shame" (1 Corinthians 15:34).

"… he that winneth souls is wise" (Proverbs 11:30).

"I must work the works of him that sent me, while it is day: the night cometh, when no man can work" (John 9:4).

David and Joy Weaver are missionaries in the Philippines. The Lord helped David write this encouraging poem:

Ode to a Missionary

He left a promising career,
She left her books and scope;
He left a ground floor business deal,
The book she never wrote.
Instead, unknown, they labored long
For one elusive prize –
To see the love of Christ
Ignite some heathen's blinded eyes.
No thanks, no shining fame, no wealth,
All dreams they left for dead;
No legacy to leave behind,
They sent it all ahead.

ABOUT THE
AUTHOR

Gertrude (Kellogg) Gammon taught in Eagle Grove, Iowa schools before going to South Africa in 1951. Thirty–one years later, she married Theodore Gammon (son of missionaries to Angola). They ministered to hospital patients in Cape Town. They returned to America in 1988 and continued visiting nursing home residents in Oklahoma, North Carolina and Iowa until Theodore went to be with the Lord in 2007.

BACK COVER PHOTO INFORMATION

Wearing beaded decorations.

Aloes in background.

"Big Grass" and baby "Pretty Country" (page 101).

"Set Alight" (page 102).

ORDER FORM

Please feel free to copy this form for your order.

To order individual copies directly from the author,
mail a copy of this form and your payment to:

Gertrude E. Gammon
1125 Elim Drive, Apt. D
Marion, IA 52302

Phone: 319-373-1880

AFRICA TREKS **$15.00 each including shipping**

Quantity _____ @ $15.00 each ....$_____

6% Sales Tax (Iowa residents only)...................$_____

TOTAL...$_____

Send To:

NAME_____

ADDRESS_____

CITY_____STATE_____ZIP_____

PHONE_____

(Retailers, please contact the publisher for ordering details.
Contact information is located in the front of the book.)